M000274967

Becoming a Mediator

Peter Lovenheim

Becoming a Mediator

An Insider's Guide to Exploring Careers in Mediation

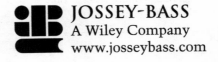

JOSSEY-BASS
A Wiley Company
www.josseybass.com

Published by

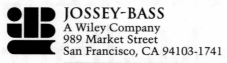

JOSSEY-BASS
A Wiley Company
989 Market Street
San Francisco, CA 94103-1741

www.josseybass.com

Jossey-Bass books and products are available through most bookstores. To contact
Jossey-Bass directly, call (888) 378-2537, fax to (800) 605-2665, or visit our website
at www.josseybass.com.

Substantial discounts on bulk quantities of Jossey-Bass books are available to corporations, professional associations, and other organizations. For details and discount information, contact the special sales department at Jossey-Bass.

We at Jossey-Bass strive to use the most environmentally sensitive paper stocks available
to us. Our publications are printed on acid-free recycled stock whenever possible, and our
paper always meets or exceeds minimum GPO and EPA requirements.

Library of Congress Cataloging-in-Publication Data

Lovenheim, Peter.
    Becoming a mediator: an insider's guide to exploring careers in mediation/
Peter Lovenheim.—1st ed.
      p. cm.
    Includes bibliographical references and index.
    ISBN 0-7879-5061-0 (alk. paper)
    1. Conflict management—Vocational guidance—United States. 2. Mediation—
Vocational guidance—United States. 3. Dispute resolution (Law)—Vocational
guidance—United States. I. Title.
HM1126+

2001008353

HB Printing   10 9 8 7 6 5 4 3 2 1   FIRST EDITION

Contents

To Jan Goldberg,
Mediator, Mentor, Mensch

Introduction

There's a cartoon I like: it shows two men in business suits seated on a park bench. Their suits are muddied and torn; they look like bums. One turns to the other and says, sadly, "We should have gone to mediation."

We're meant to understand that the two men had knocked heads together in a lawsuit, and both had been ruined. They could have been business partners, an employee and his boss, neighbors, even former friends. They could be any two people caught in a dispute—and then caught again in the adversarial legal system.

Fortunately, in recent years, increasing numbers of Americans have caught on that all conflict doesn't have to end in court. Instead, as a first resort, more and more people are trying to work out solutions to their disputes with the aid of trained, neutral third parties: mediators. Across the country, hundreds of thousands of cases have been successfully resolved through mediation. Not surprisingly, as people experience mediation, many become curious about whether they too could become mediators.

I have been involved in mediation for more than fifteen years, first as a volunteer mediator, then as a private mediator, then as owner of a dispute resolution company. In all those years, the question I have most frequently been asked—in person, on the phone, even on radio interview shows—is, "How does a person become a mediator?"

The answer, unfortunately, is never simple. As a profession, mediation is still relatively new and unformed. There is no obvious career path; there are no prescribed courses to take or degrees to earn. To build a career as a mediator requires knowledge of the field, some creativity, and lots of perseverance.

MOTIVES FOR MEDIATING

Nevertheless, more and more people every year decide to give it a try. Why is that? For the money? A few people—and some appear in the pages of this book—make $1 million a year mediating; others earn six-figure incomes. Those employed full-time with government agencies may earn $60,000 to $80,000; those in private practice may charge $50 to $250 an hour, depending on their specialty and where they live. But mediators who become rich are the exception. Most are fortunate to earn a modest income; many find that they need to supplement their practices with teaching, training, or other pursuits.

Is it for the prestige? Some prominent mediators—former president Jimmy Carter, for example—enjoy worldwide esteem for their accomplishments as peacemakers. But for the most part, mediators labor out of the limelight and receive minimal recognition for their work.

Jerome T. Barrett notes in his paper, "The Psychology of a Mediator," that the mediator is

> an outside intervenor, working under high stress on the problems of others . . . in isolation from any support groups, and bound by a strict code of confidentiality. The mediator's opportunities for positive feedback are limited, the success of his performance is difficult to measure, and he is subjected to the manipulations of the parties.[1]

I'll discuss this issue more in Chapter Four, but Barrett's point is well taken: status and prestige are only rarely the mediator's reward, so a desire for them is probably not what drives most people to this line of work.

The real motivation lies elsewhere, I think, and is more noble than a desire for wealth or recognition. It can be found in a deeply felt need to be of service, to use one's skills to accomplish something of value, to connect with other people and to make a difference in their lives.

Listen to the words of some mediators: "Most people, after doing their first mediation, levitate for a time. Your hat size grows three-fold, you feel wonderful and want to do nothing but mediate for the rest of your career." That's Mark Appel, senior vice president of the American Arbitration Association (AAA), but any of dozens of other mediators I know might say the same thing.

Or consider this from Dolly Hinkley, a divorce mediator: "I've met some really nice people from doing this work—people who are really concerned about their children and who want to do best for their spouse. . . . I like being the one to help them. I don't think I'm ever going to retire."

Or this from Chris Kauders, a lawyer-turned-mediator who, through his company Pre-Trial Solutions, Inc., in Boston, mediates personal injury and employment cases: "I love it. I love helping the parties solve the disputes. It's tiring. It can be grueling. But I love it."

Or finally, this from Don Reder, commercial mediator and president of Dispute Resolution, Inc., in Hartford, Connecticut: "I think it's the best job in the world. I love it. I hope I can keep doing it until it's time for me to check out."

Helping people end conflict is sacred work, and most mediators feel it. A few may become rich, and a handful receive wide praise, but all mediators—from the volunteer helping neighbors settle a dispute over a shared driveway, to the family mediator helping a couple cooperate for the sake of their children, to the commercial mediator helping companies preserve a business relationship—all are sustained by rewards beyond money, praise, or fame.

I can add my own testimonial. In 1986, after about seven years of practicing law, I was walking one day at lunch hour through a shopping mall when I casually picked up a flyer from an information table. It described the work of the Center for Dispute Settlement—a nonprofit community mediation center in Rochester, New York—and said the group was looking for volunteer mediators. I didn't know exactly what mediation was, but the general idea intrigued me, and I signed up for a training class. Some months later I heard my first case. I forget all the details, but it involved two neighbors, trespassing children, and property lines. After several hours, the neighbors reached an agreement, and I was hooked. The satisfaction of helping two strangers work out a solution to their problem so they and their families could put it behind them and get on with their lives was immense.

I'm pleased to be able to offer, through this book, a road map for you to follow so you can become a mediator, too. It can be a challenge to find your way in this new field, to find your niche and then to become successful. But if you persevere, in the end I'm sure you will be glad you made the journey.

As I noted, mediation is a young field and still evolving. Just as you will need to find your niche within the field, mediation is still finding its niche within our society. Some problem areas remain. You should be aware of them.

PROBLEMS IN THE FIELD

First, in some parts of the field and in some communities, it seems there are more mediators than disputes to resolve. This is an illusion. The problem isn't that there aren't enough disputes—human beings produce them in ample numbers. It's just that many in the public are still not aware of mediation as an option. Therefore, getting people to bring their disputes to mediation can be an ongoing challenge. If you work as a salaried mediator with a government program, this problem generally won't affect you; there are enough cases because more and more laws now mandate mediation for certain types of cases—employment discrimination claims, for example. If, however, you are a mediator in private practice, you may need to be constantly drumming up business in order to get enough cases through the door. As Don Reder, president of Dispute Resolution, Inc., observes:

> If you're going the independent route—setting up a practice as an independent mediator—you have to be prepared to do relentless marketing. Unfortunately, many of the people who want to get into the business don't want to do relentless marketing. But that is the reality of the field. The truth is, it's harder sometimes to get cases than to settle cases.

Another problem is the role of lawyer-mediators. In the early years of mediation—the 1970s and 1980s—the organized bar largely scoffed at mediation, as if it were an inferior and unworthy means of handling disputes. But as mediation began to catch on—and lawyers themselves gained experienced with it—the bar began to view it more favorably. Now, many lawyers have taken mediator training and make themselves available to mediate cases. They have also convinced some state courts and legislatures that, for certain types of cases coming out of the court system, only lawyers should be allowed to mediate. As a result, some state and federal government programs now either exclude nonlawyers from mediating or give preference to lawyer-mediators. Also, many lawyers, when they refer clients to mediation, have a bias in favor of choosing mediators who are themselves lawyers.

To be sure, there are times when a mediator's effectiveness is enhanced by a knowledge of the law and local legal customs. However, a legal background by itself does not make someone a good mediator. The role of lawyer-mediators is a contentious issue within the mediation field and one that is not likely to be resolved soon.

JOB OPPORTUNITIES

If you happen to be a lawyer, know that there are plenty of job opportunities available to you as a mediator. If you are not a lawyer, the good news is that you also have plenty of job opportunities, and I have made an effort throughout this book to point them out. For example, the new area of on-line mediation appears to offer especially good opportunities for mediators who are not lawyers. On-line disputes tend to concern straightforward commercial transactions rather than complex legal cases, so on-line mediation firms do not appear to favor mediators with law backgrounds as do some other private mediation firms.

And sometimes mediators may be preferred because they are *not* lawyers. Moshe Cohen, a businessman who became a mediator in Cambridge, Massachusetts, explains: "All these other attorney-mediators are connected to the legal community in ways I'm never going to be, but a lot of business people don't like lawyers and are glad to use a businessperson as a mediator if they know one."

Whatever your background—law, social work, teaching, psychology, business, homemaking, or parenting—if you have the skills and desire, I believe you can become a mediator and find a satisfying career.

OVERVIEW OF THE BOOK

This book can help you decide whether you want to become a mediator. In Chapter One, you will learn exactly what mediation is; Chapter Two explains what mediators actually do and what kinds of cases they hear. Chapter Three provides more specific information about mediators, explaining who they are and where they work; Chapter Four describes some of the personality traits common to many mediators.

And you will see, in later chapters, that there are plenty of good places to be trained in mediation (see Chapter Five), that ample jobs are available (see Chapter Six for descriptions), and that even

more jobs are available in supportive roles, such as case management, administration, and sales. Those jobs are described in Chapter Seven.

If you decide to become a mediator, I believe you will have not
only the opportunity to develop a good career but, in a society that
is increasingly fragmented and violent, you will have the personal
satisfaction of becoming a diplomat for peace. And you can use
those peacemaking skills wherever you go for the benefit of the people you care about most: people in your community, your place of
work, and your home.

I hope this book helps you begin.

January 2002   Peter Lovenheim
Rochester, New York

Acknowledgments

I'm grateful to many people for their help in preparing this book.

I want to thank Andrew Thomas, director of the Center for Dispute Settlement in Rochester, New York, for giving me the opportunity fifteen years ago to be trained as a mediator and later to join the staff. I also thank the Center's current training staff for allowing me to observe and participate in a recent training session.

Thanks also to the Office of Special Studies at the Chautauqua Institution in Chautauqua, New York, for letting me teach a course on "Becoming a Mediator" and to the students who helped me refine the ideas presented here.

I want to thank the many mediators, professors, administrators, and others who spoke with me about their work and who allowed me to include their comments in this book. They are Joan Chisholm, John Polanski, Mark Keppler, Hon. Anton J. Valukas, Hon. Leon A. Beerman, Dolly Hinckley, Joseph Grynbaum, Michael Lang, Craig Coletta, Frank Blechman, Kathy Hale, Beth Danehy, Loretta Feller, Deana Kardel, Mark Appel, Brian Jerome, Chris Kauders, Jeff Krivis, Moshe Cohen, Colin Rule, and Don Reder.

Special thanks are due Jim Melamed of Mediate.com. Jim's knowledge of the mediation field and his insight into the experience of being a mediator were of great help.

I thank Leslie Berriman, the editor who convinced me I should take the time to write this book and who helped me get started, and Lasell Whipple, who saw the project through to completion. Lasell, thank you for your patience and understanding when one of the subjects I was writing about hit too close to home.

To Jan Goldberg, former business partner and now my friend: thank you for helping me keep at it and teaching me so much about so many things.

Finally, to my children, Sarah, Val, and Ben: I wish you lives filled with contented love and homes filled with peace.

P. L.

Becoming a Mediator

1

What Is Mediation?

*T*o *mediate* means "to go between" or "to be in the middle." This, literally, is what mediators do. They go between people involved in a dispute and try to help them work out a solution to their problem.

Here is a formal definition: *Mediation is a process in which two or more people in a dispute come together to try to work out a solution to their problem with the help of a neutral third person—the mediator.*

The mediator's role is not that of a judge deciding who is right and who is wrong. Neither is it to give legal advice (even if the mediator happens to be a lawyer); nor is it to be a counselor or therapist. The mediator's only role is to bring the parties together to help them evaluate their goals and options and find their own solution to their problem.

Exactly how the mediator does this may be puzzling to those not familiar with the process. After all, each of us is at times a mediator: department heads mediate between workers; parents mediate between children; friends mediate between friends. Yet most people would not presume themselves capable of sitting down in a room with total strangers and, in the course of an hour or two, helping them find a solution to a problem that may have vexed them for months or years.

Formal mediation involves a lot more than just getting folks together to talk about their problem. It involves the mediator, who

is trained in conflict resolution, and it involves the mediation session, a highly ritualized, multistage proceeding. Employing their
skills through the different stages of mediation, mediators attempt
to unfreeze the parties from their fixed positions and open them to
the possibilities of creative solutions. The mediator works to help
the parties

- Discover the true issues involved in their dispute

- Understand the difference between what they want
  and what they need

- Understand the wants and needs of the other side

- Realistically consider the possible options

MEDIATION COMPARED TO ARBITRATION AND LITIGATION

An experienced mediator once lamented: "I spend a lot of time at
dinner parties explaining that mediation is neither arbitration nor
meditation."

People often do confuse the words *mediation, arbitration*, and
litigation—and *meditation*. I was once introduced on a national talk
show as an expert on how to resolve disputes through meditation!
Even the esteemed journal *Mediation Quarterly* published one issue
with *Meditation Quarterly* printed on the spine. But the words themselves sound more alike than the procedures they describe actually are.
Let's take a quick look at the three processes and how they differ.

LITIGATION: In litigation, parties go to court to have a judge or
jury decide their rights under the law. Parties usually hire lawyers to
guide them through the legal action and to speak for them in court.
Throughout the process, strict rules must be followed as to what
information and documents the parties may present, as well as what

they can say to try to prove their case. These are called *rules of evidence*. Typically in litigation, one side wins and the other side loses, although the losing side can ask a higher court to change the decision in what is called an *appeal*. If a court orders one side to pay money or take other actions, the order can be enforced by marshals, police, or other government agencies.

ARBITRATION: Arbitration is a little like going to a private court with more relaxed rules; it has long been used to resolve commercial and labor disputes (including, more recently, labor disputes in professional sports). In arbitration, a neutral third party—the *arbitrator*—conducts a hearing between the disputants and then, acting as a judge, renders a legally binding decision. Arbitration is less formal than litigation, and strict rules of evidence are not usually followed. Partly for this reason, cases tend to move through arbitration much more quickly than they do in court. The arbitrator's decision is usually binding and cannot be overturned except in rare circumstances, such as if the arbitrator is later found to have been biased either in favor of or against one of the parties.

MEDIATION: In mediation, the neutral mediator does not act as a judge or arbitrator; he or she has no authority to impose a decision. Instead, the mediator conducts a face-to-face hearing with the disputants and, using special skills of listening, questioning, negotiating, and creating options, helps the parties work out *their own* solution to their dispute. In effect, the mediator acts as a catalyst; the mediator's skills, acting on both parties, help them resolve their dispute.

Compromise is often involved but not in the sense of splitting the difference. The goal is to find a win-win solution in which both sides achieve something they want. Rules of evidence and other formal procedures are not normally used in mediation, but the agreement reached can be made legally binding when drafted in the form of a contract. Table 1.1 lists some of the differences among mediation, arbitration, and litigation.

Table 1.1.   Differences Among Mediation, Arbitration, and Litigation

Process	Mediation	Arbitration	Litigation
Who decides?	Parties	Arbitrator	Judge or jury
Who controls?	Parties	Arbitrator and attorneys	Judge and attorneys
Procedure	Informal	Somewhat formal	Formal
Time to hearing	Weeks	Months	Years
Cost to party	Nominal or low	Moderate	Substantial
Rules of evidence	None	Informal	Complex
Publicity	Private	Usually private	Public
Relations of parties	Cooperation may increase	Antagonistic	Antagonistic
Focus	Future	Past	Past
Method of negotiation	Compromise	Hard bargaining	Hard bargaining
Communication	Often improved	Blocked	Blocked
Goal	Win-Win	Win-Lose	Win-Lose
Compliance	Generally honored	Often resisted or appealed	Often resisted or appealed

Source: Adapted from Cloke and Strachan, "Mediation and Prepaid Legal Plans," *Mediation Quarterly,* 1987, *18,* 94.

MEDIATION IS FLEXIBLE AND FORWARD LOOKING

Courts are often limited in the kinds of disputes they can hear: bankruptcy courts hear bankruptcy cases; family courts hear family disputes. Mediation, however, is not a court; it is a process that can be applied to nearly all kinds of disputes. It can be used to decide who will own the Sinai Peninsula or who will park their car on weekends in the driveway you share with your next-door neighbor. It can be used to determine how one computer company will compensate another for infringing on the rights to use its operating system software or how your dry cleaner will compensate you for fraying the collars of your dress shirts. It can be used to determine if a shelter for the homeless can be operated by a church in a residential neighborhood in Atlanta or in whose home your children should live after you and your spouse divorce.

For these and many other types of disputes, mediation works so well because it is forward looking, not backward looking. The law looks back to find who was right and who was wrong; mediation looks ahead to find a solution both parties can live with. In law, the court uses its power to dictate a decision; in mediation, people *empower themselves* to find their own solutions.

MEDIATION IS EMPOWERING

This issue of empowerment may be a key to understanding why mediation has taken hold and is gaining so fast in popularity. Many people rightly wonder why it should take two to three years to get a result in a simple legal claim for $10,000. They wonder why, in going to court, people should tolerate an experience that may resemble, to paraphrase Jerold S. Auerbach, a sudden regression to childhood, where they can understand neither the procedures nor the language, where an attorney assumes the role of parent and the disputant becomes a dependent child, and where the judge looms as a menacing authority figure, empowered to divest litigants of property or liberty.[1]

Why not, as educated and reasonable adults, meet face-to-face with people with whom we have disputes and, with the aid of the skilled mediator, give *ourselves* the power to work out a solution to our own problem? "Mediation," notes mediator Paul Wahrhaftig, is an "attempt by everyday people to wrestle back control over their own problems."[2]

MEDIATION COMPARED TO OTHER FORMS OF DISPUTE RESOLUTION

To better understand mediation, consider where it fits among other dispute resolution techniques. In addition to arbitration and litigation, these include

- *Negotiation:* Parties try to resolve their dispute by talking directly with each other or through their counsel.

- *Conciliation:* A neutral third party intervenes, not so much to resolve the dispute as to reduce tensions and get the parties talking.

- *Fact finding:* A neutral third party—often an expert in the matter under dispute—assesses the issues and presents findings of fact and recommendations to the parties.

As disputants move from left to right on the chart shown below, generally the cost of the dispute resolution method increases while the parties' control over the process and their dispute decreases.

Negotiation   Conciliation   Fact Finding   Mediation   Arbitration   Litigation

HISTORY AND GROWTH OF MEDIATION

In eastern cultures, mediation has long been the preferred method of resolving disputes. In Japan, where there are said to be more flower arrangers than lawyers, mediation is used extensively. In China, it is estimated that thirty-five times as many disputes are settled through mediation as through the courts; some eight hundred thousand mediation panels operate at local and regional levels, with more than one million people trained as mediators.[3]

Even in the United States, mediation has a long history. In 1636, the Puritan founders of Dedham (a community located south-west of Boston) provided in their covenant for a system of informal mediation. In New Netherland, Dutch colonists established a Board of Nine Men to serve as "friendly mediators and arbitrators." In colonial Virginia, the legislature noted the "excessive charges and greate delaies"[4] of litigation and encouraged citizens to resolve disputes by other means.

Later, beginning in the 1800s, Chinese immigrants on the West Coast, Scandinavian immigrants in the Midwest, and Jewish immigrants in New York set up mediation boards to resolve disputes within their own communities. In 1947, the federal government established the Federal Mediation and Conciliation Service (FMCS) to resolve disputes between industry and labor; in 1964, the U.S. Department of Justice formed the Community Relations Service to mediate racial disputes arising under the Civil Rights Act.

The current surge of interest in mediation began in the early 1970s—a time when state and federal courts were swamped with huge numbers of lawsuits by consumers, minorities, home owners, crime victims, and so on. This rush to court, known as the *litigation explosion*, resulted in delays—sometimes of many years—before people could have their cases heard by a judge. In an early effort to address the problem, the U.S. Department of Justice conducted an experiment in three U.S. cities—Atlanta, Kansas City, and Los Angeles. The goal was to answer this question: Could disputes involving ordinary citizens be successfully resolved through mediation as an alternative to traditional litigation?

During a fifteen-month test period in the late 1970s, 3,947 disputes were handled by locally based mediation centers in the three cities. Of the cases that went to a formal mediation session, more than 82 percent were successfully resolved; as many as 95 percent were resolved for some types of disputes.[5]

Six-month follow-up interviews with the disputants showed very high rates of satisfaction with mediation, as detailed in Table 1.2. (In

Table 1.2.   Disputant Satisfaction for Mediated Cases

Question	Response	Claimant	Respondent
Satisfied with	Yes	88%	88%
mediation experience?	No	9%	8%
	Somewhat	4%	4%
Satisfied with	Yes	84%	89%
mediation process?	No	12%	10%
	Somewhat	3%	5%
Satisfied with mediator?	Yes	88%	88%
	No	8%	7%
	Somewhat	4%	5%
Satisfied with terms	Yes	80%	83%
of agreement?	No	15%	13%
	Somewhat	5%	5%

Source: Cook, Roehl, and Sheppard, *Neighborhood Justice Centers Field Test: Final Evaluation Report, Executive Summary.* Washington, D.C.: Government Printing Office, 1980, p. 15.

the table, the term *claimant* refers to the person who initiated mediation, and *respondent* refers to the party who agreed to participate.)

In telephone interviews,[6] disputants explained their attitudes about having tried mediation.

In Kansas City:

> Mr. S. described his experience with the court as lousy, as opposed to his feeling that the people at [the mediation center] were fair . . . also, cooperative and helpful, as opposed to the general lack of cooperation at the court. In court he had no say.

> Mr. R. [who had been in matrimonial court one time previously with his wife] said, in comparison to court, he felt the [mediation] people were trying to resolve his and his ex-wife's differences, whereas the court was a frightening experience.

"Going to court is a contest between lawyers, not a way of solving problems between people."

In Los Angeles:

The claimant [a businessman] was very satisfied with the process and the mediator . . . "takes less time than courts" . . . and he got his money.

Ms. M. was very positive about the whole experience. "The mediator was skillful, and the respondent lived up to the terms of the agreement. My previous court experience was scary."

In 1980, the U.S. Congress, finding that "the inadequacy of dispute resolution mechanisms throughout the United States is contrary to the general welfare of the people,"[7] passed the Dispute Resolution Act to help more local communities establish mediation centers like those that had succeeded in Atlanta, Kansas City, and Los Angeles.

As it turned out, Congress never did provide funding for more local mediation centers, but state and local governments did. In 1975, there were fewer than a dozen public mediation centers around the country, but by 1985 there were 182; today, nearly 400 centers serve U.S. communities from coast to coast, handling hundreds of thousands of cases per year. Later, we'll look more closely at these public mediation centers and what kinds of cases they handle.

In recent decades, other national legislation—the Administrative Dispute Resolution Act, for example—and scores of state laws have been passed to establish, fund, and promote the use of mediation in an ever-increasing range of circumstances.

At the same time, the private sector has spawned hundreds of national, regional, and local for-profit dispute resolution services, as well as thousands of independent private mediators. The private services tend to specialize in mediating legal and business disputes; they may charge substantial fees for their services, but the fees are nearly always far lower than the cost of litigation. Independent mediators in private practice handle everything from complex construction cases to family disputes and divorce. (For more about these and other types of mediation services, see Chapter Three.)

WHAT MEDIATION LOOKS LIKE

The bailiff bangs three times on the courtroom door and says, "All Rise! This court is now in session, the Honorable Peter Lovenheim presiding!" If I were a judge, that is how a hearing in my courtroom might begin.

Mediation begins differently: "Hello. Are you Rebecca LeClair? I'm Peter Lovenheim, the mediator. Will you follow me to the hearing room, please?"

Part of the reason for this striking difference between the courtroom and the mediation room is mediation's focus on relationships rather than formality. If the parties have a relationship with each other, that will become an important factor in the mediation process. But as we'll see later, mediators themselves must establish a trusting relationship with the parties in order to do their job effectively.

Mediation's low-key opening is deceiving because it is really just the overture to a compelling drama about to unfold. What happens most days in court, by comparison, could be considered boring. Remember, mediation is not combat by hired gun; in a mediation session, the disputants themselves—former business partners, angry neighbors, a former employee and the boss who fired her—meet nose-to-nose across the mediation table, with the chance, *at last,* to say what is on their minds.

Mediation is a process that moves from one stage to the next, giving disputants time to speak and be listened to, to meet privately with the mediator, and to work together to find a solution to their dispute.

If you've never seen a mediation, it may be difficult to picture exactly what it looks like. After all, there are no weekly television shows about the work of mediators, as there are about lawyers and judges. To understand better what mediation looks like, let's walk through a typical case of the type that might be handled at a non-profit, tax-supported public mediation center. Many mediators get their first training and experience at these centers (see Chapter Three for more details).

Where the Mediation Is Held

A mediation arranged through a public mediation center is likely to be held at the center's own offices, typically in a downtown office or civic building. It will probably be a bare-bones conference room, with pale green walls and a wobbly, wood-veneer table with folding metal chairs. Mediations arranged by local and state courts, by contrast, are usually held in conference rooms at the courthouse. When mediations are arranged by private dispute resolution companies, the setting can be plush, such as in a big law firm's conference room.

Length of Session

Most small, two-party cases—neighborhood disputes, consumer claims, minor business disputes—are mediated in a half day—at most in a full day. Multiparty cases last longer, as do major commercial disputes such as complex contract and construction disputes; they may last several days, either all in a row or scheduled over a period of weeks. Divorce mediation generally requires a half-dozen sessions, usually spread over several months.

Some mediation programs are run by court systems, which I'll discuss later, but it's worth noting that these programs frequently impose time limits on mediation. A two-hour limit, with the option to continue another day if the mediation appears to be productive, would be typical.

Agreement to Mediate

Ideally, people involved in a dispute will decide together to try mediation. In reality this seldom happens. Usually, by the time one side is thinking about the need for mediation, the relationship is so strained that neither is talking to the other. Common procedure, therefore, is for one side to initiate mediation by contacting a mediation service. The person is asked to complete a brief Submission to Mediation form containing the names and contact information of the parties and a brief description of the dispute. The service takes over from there.

Next a case manager at the mediation service contacts the other side (now designated the *respondent*), usually by mail. Occasionally, respondents readily agree to mediate, but more often they are reluctant. Sometimes they may have good reason to refuse. An example of what a good reason might be is this: if they are likely to win in court and have the money and time to see the case through to a verdict. More often, however, respondents hesitate because (1) mediation is unfamiliar and therefore threatening or (2) they feel so much hostility they can't stomach the idea of sitting in the same room with their opponent, or (3) a lawyer who is unfamiliar with mediation or who has a negative attitude about it has advised against it. A lawyer might say, for example, "Oh, this mediation business isn't for you. Ignore it. If the other side's serious, let them file suit and then we'll deal with it."

Good case managers spend as much time as necessary with respondents to try to overcome their fears or objections to mediation. Often this can require many rounds of phone calls and negotiations concerning exactly what issues will be mediated, who the mediator will be, and when and where the session will be held.

If and when both sides agree to participate, they will be asked to sign an Agreement to Mediate. This brief document (typically a single page) names the parties and the selected mediator and commits the parties to participate in mediation at the agreed-on time and place, in accordance with the rules and procedures of the mediation service. (For an example of a typical set of mediation rules, see Resource A.)

Here is a sample of an Agreement to Mediate that is used at a private dispute resolution company.

AGREEMENT TO MEDIATE

Empire Mediation & Arbitration, Inc.

The undersigned agree to have Empire Mediation & Arbitration, Inc. ("Empire") provide mediation services for their dispute.

PURPOSE & RULES: Mediation is a voluntary process in which the mediator assists the parties in finding mutually agreeable settlement terms. The mediator does not have authority to impose a decision or to give legal advice. The hearing is conducted in accordance with Empire's "Commercial Mediation Rules."

MEDIATOR: The parties agree that James C. Moore, Esq., will be the sole Mediator in this case. The Mediator is an independent contractor, not an agent or employee of Empire.

AUTHORITY TO SETTLE: The parties affirm they have authority to act on behalf of the persons or organizations they represent.

FEES: Parties agree to pay mediation fees to Empire in accordance with the attached fee agreement.

LEGAL COUNSEL: Parties have the right to legal counsel and are encouraged to obtain legal advice in connection with this case.

CONFIDENTIALITY: Mediation is strictly confidential and constitutes a settlement negotiation. Statements made are inadmissible, as allowed by law, in future arbitration or court proceedings relating to this dispute. The parties will keep the confidentiality of the mediation and not introduce in any later proceeding statements made by the mediator or the parties, or subpoena a mediator to testify or produce records.

_____   _____
Name of Party   Attorney or Representative

Dated: _____

Who Attends

The people who are directly involved in the dispute are the ones who must attend mediation: the neighbors fighting over noise, the boss and the former employee she terminated, the homeowner and the electrician who did the allegedly faulty wiring. In divorce mediation, of course, it is the husband and wife who meet directly with the mediator.

When parties other than individuals are involved, such as government agencies, insurance companies, or other corporations, it is essential that somebody at the table for each side have authority to settle. Otherwise, hours of effort in mediation can be for nothing. An alternative is to have someone from company headquarters, for example, be available by telephone to approve the terms of a proposed settlement.

People always have the right to bring a lawyer to mediation, but in most interpersonal disputes and small-business cases, lawyers are not necessary and only increase the cost of the process for the participants. Sometimes, instead of bringing lawyers, parties in these smaller cases bring a friend or relative for moral support and to remind them to raise certain issues. In cases involving substantial money or legal rights, it is common for lawyers to attend, although the lawyers who really understand how mediation works let their clients do much of the talking and function more as advisers than advocates.

Witnesses, for the most part, are not needed because the point of mediation is not to determine what happened in the past but what is going to happen in the future to resolve the dispute. Nevertheless, if parties want to bring witnesses they certainly may; witnesses generally attend only part of the session, say what they need to, and then leave.

Physical Setting

The mediator typically greets the parties in a waiting area, conducts them into the conference room, and invites them to take a seat at the table.

Exactly what is the perfect shape for a mediation table? This is a subject mediators debate vigorously in the pages of professional journals. Some prefer a rectangular table because they believe its resemblance to a typical boardroom table inspires confidence in the mediation process; others dislike the rectangular table because they think the hard lines encourage hard and inflexible bargaining positions. Some like a square table on the theory that its four equal sides suggest equality among the parties. Still others prefer no table at all and, instead, like to have the disputants sit in upholstered armchairs around a coffee table or on a comfortable sofa facing the mediator.

The mediator sits at the head of the table. Parties sit on opposite sides with lawyers and witnesses, if any, seated beside them.

What the Mediator Knows

Disputants normally will have submitted a short memorandum to the mediator before the session, briefly stating what the case is about and what they hope to get out of it. In this way, the mediator already knows something about the dispute and, if necessary, has been able to brush up on the subject—home construction, employment law, or whatever—before the session begins.

At public mediation centers, however, where mostly interpersonal disputes and small consumer claims are heard, often the parties do not submit a prehearing memo. The mediator does not meet with the parties individually before meeting with them together, so without a prehearing memo, the session begins with the mediator having little knowledge of the parties other than their names, addresses, and a brief description of the type of dispute.

STAGES OF THE MEDIATION SESSION

To understand what happens in mediation, it is helpful to think of the process as divided into distinct stages. By convention, most mediators speak of the process as being divided into six stages. Each of these stages is discussed, in order, in the sections that follow.

Stage One: The Mediator's Opening Statement

As the mediation session begins, the mediator has no need to get the disputants' attention because, typically, no one is speaking. Often it is the first time they have seen each other in weeks or months. Now they sit silently across the table, staring at the mediator.

The first lines in this drama are the mediator's and are known as the *opening statement*. This is a short speech, usually delivered without notes, through which the mediator explains the goals, procedures, and rules of the session. (For a sample set of rules for mediation, see Resource A.)

The opening remarks shown next are appropriate for a dispute among neighbors at a public mediation center; they are essentially the same as I would use if mediating most other types of disputes.

Introduce Self. Good morning, my name is Peter Lovenheim. I'm the mediator for your case today.

Introduce Parties. Before we go any further, I want to make sure I have everyone's correct name and address. On my left is Rebecca LeClair of 123 Monroe Avenue. Ms. LeClair, you are the claimant in this mediation. And on my right is Arthur Wu, 43 Hilton Place. Mr. Wu, you are the respondent.

Commend Parties. I want to commend each of you for choosing mediation as a way to resolve your dispute. By doing so, you have the opportunity to solve this problem in a cooperative rather than an adversarial way and with greater flexibility, speed, and privacy than you would likely have in court.

State Goal. The Center for Dispute Settlement is a nonprofit organization set up to help people in our community resolve their disputes through mediation. Our goal in this mediation is to find a solution to your problem that will be fair to both of you and workable in the long run. Our experience is that disputants who work in good faith during mediation have a very high success rate in reaching an agreement. My job is to help you do that.

Explain Mediator's Role. As a mediator, I've been trained and certified by this Center to mediate disputes such as yours. I have no authority to render a decision, and I can't send anyone to jail or impose any fines.

I understand from the papers you submitted to start this case that you are neighbors and have some problems about noise, and perhaps some other matters. But beyond that, I have no knowledge of the dispute and no vested interest in how it is resolved. My only job is to help you find your own solution. I am completely neutral. I don't know either of you, and I have no financial, social, or other connections to either of you.

Explain the Lack of Time Pressure. One of the advantages of mediation is that we are under no time pressure. This room is available to us for as long as we want it, and I am prepared to stay here as long as the mediation appears to be productive. If, as we go along, you want to take a break for a cold drink or a stretch, just let me know and we'll do that.

Explain Procedure. We'll begin today by having each of you make an opening statement to tell us what this dispute is all about from your point of view. Ms. LeClair, as the claimant, will go first, and then Mr. Wu will have his turn. While one of you is speaking, the other one will not be allowed to interrupt. If you want to make comments later, there are pads and pencils on the table you can use to make notes. While each of you is speaking, you may notice me taking notes. If I write something, it doesn't mean I agree or disagree with what is being said. I'm taking notes just to help keep track of the facts of the case.

Explain the Use of Evidence. While you are speaking, you can show anything in the way of evidence you have brought with you, such as bills, letters, or photographs. The purpose of evidence is to help us understand your side of the dispute, not to prove who was right and who was wrong. The rules of evidence followed in court that say some information is allowed to be shown and some isn't are not followed here, so I am willing to look at anything you want to show me. The other side will be able to look at it, too.

Describe the Discussion Stage. After opening statements, we'll begin to discuss the issues and hear from any witnesses you have brought. During this discussion phase, you can each say whatever you like, but I won't allow any uncivil language or swearing.

Mention Possibility of Caucusing. At some point I may want to talk with each of you separately in what is called a *caucus*. If that happens, I will ask one of you to leave the room while I speak with the other. Everything you tell me in a caucus I will keep confidential and not tell the other side, unless you give me specific permission to do so. If I spend longer in caucus with one side than the other, it doesn't mean I am partial to one side; it just means it may be taking me a little longer to understand the facts and options available.

Stress Confidentiality. You have both signed a pledge to keep everything said and revealed in this mediation confidential. (This pledge appears in the Agreement to Mediate, shown earlier, that the parties signed before the session.) The Standards of Conduct for Mediators (see Resource B) requires that I also keep what you say and show me confidential.

Describe Consent Agreement. As I said, our goal today is to find a solution to your dispute that both of you feel is fair and workable in the long run. If we can find such a solution, I will help you write it up in what we call a *consent agreement*. This will be an official document you will sign and we will have notarized. It will be a binding contract and may be legally enforceable in court. (In disputes involving large sums of money, property, or legal rights, the parties often want a lawyer or business adviser to review an agreement before signing.)

Invite Questions. Before we begin with your opening statements, are there any questions? If not, then Ms. LeClair, you are the claimant, so let's begin with you. Please tell us what this case is all about.

Besides explaining how the mediation session will be conducted, mediators use the opening remarks to help achieve their first and perhaps most important goal: to gain control of the session. They have control at the start, of course, but that is mostly because the parties don't quite know what to expect and are being polite. The first time one side calls the other a liar or a disgrace to the neighborhood, things may quickly get out of hand. What is to prevent the session from degenerating into a shouting match or gripe session where nothing is accomplished?

The way the mediator keeps control as a session moves ahead is by earning the trust, respect, and confidence of the parties. He does this by the way he conducts himself. From the first meeting with the parties, everything the mediator says and does is designed with this goal in mind. When the mediator greets the parties in the waiting area, he presents a neat appearance and speaks politely and respectfully. During the opening statement, he speaks confidently, answers the parties' questions fully, and otherwise tries to demonstrate intelligence, knowledge, and neutrality—in short, showing he is someone in whom the parties can and should place their trust.

Stage Two: The Parties' Opening Statements

When the mediator is done with opening remarks, the parties are invited to make their own statements. For a disputant (either claimant or respondent), this is a rare chance, finally and without interruption, to tell the other side and the mediator what the dispute looks like from his or her own point of view. Consider how delicious this opportunity is. Even if a party has tried before mediation to negotiate a settlement directly with the other side, he has probably never had the chance to tell his side of the story without being interrupted or having to shout. Even in court, disputants probably would not get such a chance until the case came to trial and they were called to testify. But chances are they would be interrupted by objections from opposing counsel and required to limit their testimony to the narrow legal issues in dispute.

In mediation, the disputant now has the floor. No one will stop her. No one will object or try to twist her words. If the other side interrupts to shout, "No, she's lying!," the mediator will stop the interruption.

While the parties are making their opening statements, they may have the feeling that no one outside family and closest friends has ever listened to them quite as attentively or with as much understanding as the mediator is listening to them now. This is because mediators use the parties' opening statements not only to learn the facts of the case but to show they are good listeners. They show that they care about the parties' problems. And not only do they care and understand the problem but they understand the parties' emotional reactions to the problem. This is called *empathic listening*—an important skill mediators use to help build the parties' trust in them and in the mediation process.

Professors Nancy H. Rogers and Richard A. Salem write:

> Empathic listening means listening for how the parties feel as well as to what they are saying, and providing verbal and nonverbal (eye contact, facial expression, body position) feedback that lets them know the mediator understands and cares about both. An empathic mediator conveys respect to the parties, doesn't register approval or disapproval of what is being said,

refrains from providing unsolicited advice and does not interrupt.[8]

Stage Three: Discussion

After opening statements, it is time for the parties to start talking directly to each other. The mediator may begin by simply trying to discuss in general terms the various issues in dispute and attempt to put them in some kind of order. A common practice is to tackle the easiest ones first in order to build the disputants' confidence in the mediation process and in their own ability to address their dispute in a reasonable and productive way.

This is also a time for first narrowing and then broadening the scope of the mediation. For example, the mediator may try to narrow the number of issues in dispute: Can any complaints discussed in the opening statements be dismissed because they are no longer relevant or were simply based on misinformation? Do any issues raised need to be broadened to include underlying problems, such as hidden interpersonal conflicts, not disclosed by the parties?

Disputants often do not reveal to the mediator an important issue in their dispute, either because they do not want to or because they honestly do not recognize it. In disputes between business partners, for example, it is often easier for the parties to focus on nuts-and-bolts business matters like sales, profits, and control than it is to examine underlying personal issues such as career goals, personal financial needs, self-image, and pride. By gentle questioning and careful listening, a skilled mediator can often find clues to underlying issues, even when the parties will not or cannot raise them. It is also during this discussion stage that the parties can question each other or have witnesses speak.

Stage Four: Caucus

The caucus is "the guts" of the mediation process. It is a private meeting or series of meetings between the mediator and each party individually. In caucus, the mediator can talk with a party more informally and more candidly than he could with the other side present. During a caucus is when the business of working out a settlement usually gets done.

Usually the mediator asks one side to leave the conference room and wait in the reception area while he caucuses with the other side. Or the mediator may have one side move into a second conference room, and the mediator shuttles back and forth from one room to the other, meeting separately with each side.

Typically, the mediator caucuses with each side several times during the course of mediation. In a relatively simple two-party case—for example, one involving an auto accident or minor business dispute—it would be typical for a mediator to caucus two or three times with each side during a half-day mediation. A mediation that lasts a full day may involve three to five caucuses with each side. But there is no rule on this. The frequency of caucusing depends entirely on the mediator's style and assessment of whether caucusing is productive.

Confidentiality is essential to the success of caucusing. The mediator must keep everything said during caucus confidential unless the party clearly tells him he may reveal it to the other side.

During caucus, the mediator may probe to find additional facts about the dispute that may reveal underlying issues. What does each side really want? What is their bottom line? The mediator may be an "agent of reality" and point out weaknesses in one side's positions in order to create doubt and help bring expectations in line with reality. The mediator may also challenge each side to think of new options for settlement and ask some thought-provoking questions:

If you were in the other person's shoes, how would you feel?

What do you think is the strongest part of the other side's position?

What is the weakest part of your position?

What will you do if you do not reach an agreement?

Do you think someone who didn't know you would see you as being entirely without fault in this dispute?

If this case went to trial, is it realistic to think a jury would find the other side 100 percent in the wrong?

I've heard you say what you *want* out of this case, but what do you really *need?*

If the other side were to agree to your last proposal, how workable do you think it would be in the long run?

How much will not reaching an agreement today cost you?

If this case doesn't settle, how long might it take to get into court?

If you won in court, could the other side appeal? How long might that leave you in a state of financial uncertainty?

What are some fair ways of settling this problem—fair to you and to the other side?

How would it feel to walk away just now, with this whole matter settled?

Some of the most important questions the mediator asks during caucus are those beginning with "What if?" In other words, the mediator poses the terms of hypothetical settlements: "What if your opponent did X? Would you do Y?"

People caught up in a conflict often get stuck seeing it from only one direction. An important part of the mediator's job is to help the parties think of new ways to resolve their dispute. Here are seven options for resolving disputes that mediators often try to help the parties apply to their case.

1. *Offer a compromise:* Each side moves a little toward the middle.

2. *Offer an apology:* One side provides an official, written apology for past errors.

3. *Make an exception:* One party bends the rules a bit to settle this one case, with the understanding that it will not set a precedent for future cases.

4. *Go beyond the contract:* In order to create a win-win solution, both sides agree to do things that were not part of their original contract.

5. *Create a staged agreement:* This method helps build trust: Party A will do this, then Party B will do that, after which Party A will do another thing, and then Party B will do another thing.

6. *Create an interim agreement:* The parties agree to try something for a set time and to meet again at a definite date to evaluate the results.

7. *Agree on a partial settlement:* The parties settle what they can now, and leave the rest for later.

Stage Five: Joint Negotiations

If caucusing has been successful, the parties at this stage may be focused on a narrower range of issues; they may be forward looking and searching for settlement terms that will satisfy both their own and the other side's real needs. At this point, the mediator may bring both sides back together in the same room to resume joint discussions.

The relationship between disputants often changes at this point. Not only has their negotiation style moved from competitive to more collaborative, their perceptions of each other are more realistic. Mediator Anne Richan has compared this stage of the hearing to "watching a wall come down brick by brick, as the disputants confront each other with all the things that have been bothering them and discover that the other is not an inhuman tormentor."[9]

If the parties are able to conduct their own negotiations, the mediator will take a less active role and listen to be sure that

- Negotiations stay focused on the real issues in dispute

- No new issues emerge that may need to be addressed before negotiations proceed

- Discussion does not start down a path that may lead to an unworkable settlement (for example, one that would require a party to do something unlawful or go beyond his power to deliver)

It is also during this stage that many, but not all, mediators intervene to discourage the parties from settling their dispute on terms that the mediator believes may be unfair to one side. In divorce mediation, for example, when one spouse may be stronger psychologically or have more financial knowledge, most mediators would intervene against an unfair settlement. But in nonfamily disputes, particularly business disputes, most mediators do not see their role as protecting either side.

Stage Six: Closure

Closure occurs at the moment when both sides say yes to the same proposal. Mediation sessions tend to speed up as this point nears; everyone is familiar with the issues, so a kind of shorthand language develops that helps the discussion move to a conclusion. The mediator is also more direct in suggesting refinements to possible terms of settlement.

The mediator listens carefully to detect the first instance when a package of terms for settlement emerges from negotiations. The mediator tries to recall everything said during the session to be sure no underlying issues threaten the agreement. The mediator considers whether the settlement strikes a good balance between being specific enough to cover reasonably foreseeable problems but not so overly detailed that it would become too cumbersome to be workable.

When the mediator hears both sides say OK, it's time to seize the moment.

"Then we have agreement," says the mediator.

Closure.

WRITING THE AGREEMENT

It's important that the parties leave with something in writing that spells out the terms of their agreement. A written agreement can help make sure parties live up to the terms of their settlement. If a case is heard at a public mediation center, typically the mediator will draft the agreement while the parties wait and have them sign it before they leave. Each goes home with a copy. In more complex disputes, where parties may want to have an attorney, accountant, or other adviser review an agreement before signing, the mediator often drafts an outline of the key terms for the parties to take with them when they leave.

Typically, the settlement agreement is a short document, written in plain English so everyone can understand it, spelling out what the parties have agreed to do in order to resolve their dispute. An important point: it does not say who was guilty or at fault for past problems. The agreement is entirely forward looking, stating in clear terms who has agreed to do what and when in order to resolve the matter. If the parties wish, the agreement can be written in the form of a legal contract so that if one side fails to live up to it, the other can sue for breach of contract to have it enforced or be compensated. How to draft agreements in this form is beyond the scope of this book but is typically covered in mediator training.

Following are examples of two typical settlement agreements, each adapted from actual cases. Identifying information has been altered in order to protect the confidentiality of the parties.

The first agreement concerns a neighborhood dispute heard at a community mediation center. The case involved two families who were next-door neighbors, the Jordons and the Greens. At one time the families, each of which had young children, were friendly, but then tension developed between them. The Jordons complained that Cynthia Green's three children (she is a single mother) often came into their yard uninvited to use their play equipment and left clothes, food wrappers, toys, and other items in the yard. They also complained that Ms. Green's house guests often parked in a way that blocked their driveway. For her part, Ms. Green complained that the Jordons had made verbal threats against her and her visitors. This agreement was drafted by the two sides with the help of the mediator; the parties signed the agreement before they left the mediation center.

THE CENTER FOR
DISPUTE SETTLEMENT, INC.

In the Matter of Mediation Between:
Cynthia Green vs. Daniel and Leslie Jordon
Case Number: C-352–01

Under the Rules and Procedures of The Center for Dispute Settlement, Inc., Cynthia Green and Daniel and Leslie Jordon agree that the following provisions constitute full satisfaction of all claims submitted to Mediation on July 3, 2001.

1. Daniel and Leslie Jordon agree that Ms. Green's children and their friends can play on the swing set and other play equipment in the Jordon's backyard at any time they wish as long as they are supervised by an adult.
2. Cynthia Green agrees that her children and their friends will clean up after themselves when they play in the Jordon's yard and that she will be responsible for seeing that they do.
3. Ms. Green further agrees to tell her visitors not to park in or block the Jordon's driveway and that she will be responsible for seeing that they do not block the driveway.
4. Mr. and Mrs. Jordon agree not to make any verbal threats to Ms. Green or her visitors and to contact her directly in person or by phone if they have any complaints about the conduct of guests at her home.
5. Ms. Green and Mr. and Mrs. Jordon also agree that if future disputes arise between them, they will try to resolve them by talking together. If they are unable to do so, they will return to mediation.

If any dispute arises out of this agreement or its performance that Cynthia Green and Daniel and Leslie Jordon cannot resolve themselves, they will try to settle the dispute by mediation through the Center for Dispute Settlement, Inc.

Signature	Signature	Signature
Cynthia Green	Leslie Jordon	(Mediator's name)
	Daniel Jordon	

The next settlement agreement is from a commercial dispute that arose when a large manufacturing company, Abel Corp., claimed machine parts made for it by a smaller firm, ISN, Inc., were defective. Abel Corp. refused further delivery of parts half-way through the contract. In response, ISN claimed the parts conformed perfectly to the specifications in the purchase order and threatened to sue Abel for the actual cost of making the rejected parts. ISN was reluctant to sue, however, because Abel was a major customer; winning the lawsuit while losing Abel's business would not be in ISN's long-term interest.

The mediation took about four days over a period of three weeks. A brief outline of the agreement's main points was drafted at the last mediation session; the final version was signed a few weeks later, after attorneys for both sides had reviewed it and worked out the details. Note the total absence of fault finding. As is typical of settlement agreements, the language is entirely forward looking in order to help preserve both companies' business relationship to their mutual advantage.

SUMMARY OF
MEDIATED AGREEMENT

1. Abel Corp. agrees to award to ISN, Inc., within six months from the signing of a final mediation agreement, a contract or contracts for the manufacture of unspecified machine parts with a net profit margin to ISN upon successful completion of not less than $200,000. Counsel for the parties will draft a document further describing the parties' rights and obligations concerning this agreement for future manufacturing work.

2. Abel will pay to ISN, Inc., not later than 30 days from the signing of a final mediation agreement the amount of $600,000 to offset part of the costs incurred by ISN, Inc. to manufacture machine parts under the disputed contract, which was the subject of this mediation. Full or partial payments of this amount made after the 30-day period will include interest at the rate of 9 percent per year.

3. As further offset against ISN's manufacturing costs, Abel will purchase from ISN three Model X7 Impurities Testers for a total price of $600,000. Delivery will be made FOB Abel's East Ridge facility within 60 days following the signing of a final mediation agreement. Abel will pay ISN in full for this equipment within 30 days of satisfactory delivery.

4. ISN agrees that when the steps outlined in items 1–3 are completed, it will consider all issues concerning the disputed contract to have been settled and will not in the future bring any legal actions against Abel concerning that contract.

5. The parties will prepare and exchange papers releasing each other from all present legal claims when the steps outlined in items 1–3 are completed.

ISN, INC.

By _____

Abel CORP.

By _____

_____

Mediator

IF NO AGREEMENT IS REACHED

Although most cases settle in mediation, some do not. That's not necessarily a reflection on the mediator; some particularly thorny cases—and some particularly thorny disputants—are just not able to reach an agreement, despite the best efforts of the best mediators. If no agreement is reached, the parties have several options: they can adjourn the session and agree to come back later and try again; if the case was referred to mediation by a judge, the mediator can send the parties back to court; if the case has never been to court, one party can sue the other.

One attractive option for parties whose cases do not settle in mediation is arbitration. In arbitration, both sides tell their story to the arbitrator, and the arbitrator renders a decision. In this way, arbitration offers finality; the arbitrator's decision, called an award, is usually legally binding and enforceable by a judge.

Sometimes the parties may want the mediator to "change hats" and arbitrate a decision for them. This poses some problems, particularly if the mediator has received confidential information from the parties during caucus. But it is possible, if the parties agree to it in writing, for a mediator to turn around and arbitrate the same case. The procedure is known as *med-arb*. To avoid conflicts, however, it is more typical for the parties simply to start fresh with a new person acting as a neutral arbitrator.

The mediation procedures we've examined in this chapter can be applied successfully to all kinds of disputes. In the next chapter, we'll consider the almost unlimited variety of cases mediators handle.

2

What Kinds of Cases Do Mediators Hear?

The scope of cases that theoretically can be mediated is as extensive as the scope of human relations: from neighbors arguing
over a barking dog to countries on the brink of war. But for various
reasons, not all disputes capable of being mediated end up at the
mediation table.

In this chapter, we consider what kinds of cases mediators actually hear, the factors that favor or oppose use of mediation in any
particular case, and what makes a case well timed for mediation.

CASE VARIETY

Mediators, of course, are required to keep confidential the cases they
hear. But get into a room with several mediators, and it won't be
long before you start hearing stories (names and other essential
details withheld or changed) about the oddest, the biggest, the sad-
dest, or the most puzzling cases they've ever handled:

> "I had a case where these two sisters were arguing over their
> mother's French chateau. . . . "

> "That's nothing. I had a case where these two guys who owned
> a plastic bottle factory each claimed his own son should take
> over the business. . . . "

"Wait a minute! Did I ever tell you about the case I had about this guy who drove into his neighbor's gazebo?"

The point is that it's hard to say just what kinds of cases mediators typically handle; they typically handle every kind of case with every kind of wrinkle and odd twist. But to put some kind of frame around the picture, it may be helpful to consider the types of cases mediators hear within three broad categories: (1) interpersonal disputes, (2) commercial matters, and (3) public policy issues. Each category is discussed in the sections that follow.

Interpersonal Relations

Mediation works especially well with disputes between individuals, particularly when long-term family, work, or neighborhood relationships are involved. The mediator can help the parties reach below the surface of a dispute to address underlying issues that stress the relationship. The process allows the parties to find ways to relate to each other, even if the break can never be repaired. Examples of these types of cases include

SEPARATION AND DIVORCE: Divorcing couples mediate issues involving money, property, and children, thus saving on legal fees and also building enough trust to continue parenting their children. The same process is used by unmarried couples, including gay and lesbian couples, to resolve matters as a relationship ends.

INTACT RELATIONSHIPS: As an alternative to couples therapy or marriage counseling, couples in an otherwise intact marriage or relationship mediate specific problems in dispute, such as disagreements over child rearing, finances, in-laws, religious practices, and other family obligations.

GENERAL FAMILY RELATIONS: These cases typically involve disputes between spouses, siblings, or relatives concerning behavior, money, and inheritances. Other situations involve family members working in a family business and parents mediating relationship disputes with teenagers or adult children.

BUSINESS PARTNER RELATIONS: Co-owners of a business come to mediate issues such as sharing responsibilities within the firm, determining direction or strategy for growth, resolving conflicts in management style, and negotiating terms of an agreement if one partner wants to buy the other out.

SCHOOL ISSUES: These cases involve disputes between or among administrators, teachers, students, and parents on matters including academic standards, work conditions, class placement, and favoritism. (For more on school-based mediation, see Chapter Seven.)

WORKSITE RELATIONS: Issues for mediation among management and staff include work assignments, wrongful termination, job discrimination, and sexual harassment. (For more on work-based mediation, see Chapter Six.)

ROOMMATE RELATIONS: College students or adults in shared housing may mediate disputes involving finances, privacy, cleanliness, guests, and noise.

NEIGHBOR RELATIONS: These cases often include matters such as noise, shared driveways, pets, up-keep, and the behavior of children.

Commercial Disputes

In commercial cases, the main issue is often how much money or property is going to change hands between the parties. The parties, perhaps a merchant and a long-time customer, might have a long-term relationship, or they may be strangers—for example, two motorists in a collision. Mediation is often effective in commercial cases because in working out settlement terms, the parties can be creative and go beyond the strict terms of any legal contract that is involved. Also, both sides can confide their bottom-line needs to the mediator, who is then in a position to help them work out a mutually satisfying agreement. Examples include

SMALL CLAIMS: These are often claims by a consumer for compensation from a merchant for inadequate goods or services. Other cases include claims by merchants for monies due from a customer.

LANDLORD-TENANT DISPUTES: Tenants mediate demands for improvements to living conditions or return of security deposits. Landlords typically seek overdue rent, improvement in a tenant's behavior, or compensation for damage done to the property.

PERSONAL INJURIES: These cases usually come to mediation when someone has been injured in a car or other accident, and the insurance company initially declines to pay what the person thinks the injuries are worth.

CONTRACT DISPUTES: Owners of businesses mediate cases involving many millions of dollars in which claims of breach of contract arise from the manufacture of inadequate goods, negligent construction, or interference with customers. Often these mediations involve multiple parties.

The lists that follow illustrate the variety of disputes regularly taken to mediation and the differences in case mix between a typical community mediation center and a private dispute resolution company. Matrimonial cases—a staple for many mediators—do not appear on this list because they typically are not handled by community mediation centers. (For more on the different types of places mediators work, see Chapter Three.)

Public Policy Disputes

A host of interesting issues growing out of communitywide disputes have been successfully mediated. These include determining the siting of factories, highways, and new tract homes; how close a homeless shelter will be allowed to a residential neighborhood; what type

Top Ten Case Types Handled by Community Dispute Resolution Centers, New York State, 1999–2000

1. Breach of Contract
2. Harassment
3. Interpersonal
4. Landlord/Tenant
5. Personal and Real Property
6. Assault
7. Noise
8. Criminal Mischief
9. Behavior/Truancy
10. Fraud/Bad Check

Note: Each of forty-one counties in New York State has its own nonprofit community mediation center.

Top Ten Case Types Handled in 2000 by Empire Mediation & Arbitration, Inc.

1. Personal Injury Claims (auto accident-related)
2. Contract
3. Construction
4. Separation and Divorce
5. Employment Termination
6. Family Relationships
7. Environmental
8. Employee-to-Employee Relations
9. Property Damage
10. Health Care

Note: Empire Mediation & Arbitration, Inc., is a private dispute resolution company based in Rochester, New York.

of watercraft may use local waterways and at what speeds; and which organizations may march in a town's official Memorial Day Parade.

Regional disputes have included the competing claims to land of Native American tribes and state and county governments; disputed border claims between states; and multistate disputes over water rights.

Mediators also hear international political disputes, such as those involving conflicts among the states of the former Yugoslavia and countries in the Middle East. Among the best known and probably most successful international mediation efforts was that conducted by former president Jimmy Carter in 1978 between Prime Minister Menachem Begin of Israel and President Anwar Sadat of Egypt. Carter's thirteen-day mediation effort at Camp David, the secluded presidential retreat in the Maryland countryside, resulted in the signing of a peace agreement between those two countries that still stands today.

It is conceivable that a skilled mediator could handle almost any type of case because the process of mediation is more or less the same regardless of the type of dispute. In practice, however, mediators tend to specialize in one or more types of cases. For example, mediators with strong interpersonal skills and perhaps a background in social work or psychology might specialize in divorce and family mediation or mediation of disputes between business partners. Similarly, a mediator who is also a real estate lawyer might specialize in the mediation of disputes involving commercial or residential real estate. It would be unusual for the same mediator who hears commercial real estate disputes to also mediate divorces.

FACTORS FAVORING AND OPPOSING MEDIATION

We've considered the broad range of cases that can be heard by a mediator, but whether any particular case can or should go to mediation is another question. Certainly, if disputants seek a quick, fair, inexpensive, and flexible solution to their dispute, mediation is often the best bet. But sometimes mediation may not meet the needs of one or more of the parties, or it may be impractical in a particular case (see Table 2.1).

Following is a discussion of twelve factors often involved in determining whether any particular case will actually get mediated. Six of these factors tend to favor bringing a case to mediation, and six oppose mediation.[1]

Factors Favoring Mediation

As we have seen, mediation offers many advantages, particularly as compared to litigation, as a forum for resolving most types of disputes. The following six factors reflect some of mediation's strongest benefits, such as speed, privacy, flexibility, and cost savings. When these factors are present in a case, and people know about mediation as an option, in my experience they will readily choose to try mediation.

When Direct Negotiations Have Been Tried Without Success or Are Not Desired or Possible. In most disputes, if parties can work things out by negotiating directly with each other, that is the quickest, least expensive, and most private way to resolve the matter. If, however, direct talks have been tried and have failed, then mediation becomes an attractive next step.

Sometimes negotiations never get started. For example, one side may be ready to negotiate but can't get the attention of the other side sufficiently to start the process. This can happen when the other side is a large company or government agency that has a policy of not

Table 2.1. Pros and Cons of Mediation

Factors Favoring Mediation	Factors Opposing Mediation
Having negotiations fail	Wanting test case
Having no legal remedy	Wanting the jackpot
Preserving a relationship	One party being absent or incompetent
Maintaining privacy	One party not wanting to settle
Avoiding high fees	Finding that a serious crime is involved
Avoiding delays	Preventing immediate harm

negotiating with individuals. In this situation, a formal offer to mediate, especially if made through a respected mediation service, may be enough to get the other side's attention.

Similarly, if one party has poor negotiating skills and knows it, she might want to go directly to mediation. The mediator's presence can create a safer environment for discussion, and the mediator can help the first party get her ideas across to the other side. In this sense, mediation provides a structure for parties who have trouble dealing with each other directly to negotiate.

When the Law Cannot Provide a Remedy. Although there are thousands of laws on the books, many common disputes raise no claims for which the law provides a remedy. Disputes between family members and between neighbors are often of this type. For example, two sisters who owned and ran a jewelry store disagreed about who should control different aspects of the business. If they could not come to terms, the business might fail. Yet there were no legal claims involved—just a dispute between partners that mediation could help settle. In mediation, the more outgoing sister agreed to take on most responsibility for customer service and marketing, and the sister with more technical skills agreed to oversee purchases, manufacturing, and repairs.

Similarly, when a suburban homeowner found that lights around his neighbor's pool shone in his window at night, the law offered no solution because no local ordinance regulated outdoor residential lighting. With the help of a mediator, however, the parties were able to sit down and work out an agreement. In this case, the pool owner agreed to reposition some of her lights so they didn't shine toward the neighbor's window and to turn off others after specified hours on weekdays and weekends.

When the Parties Want to End a Problem, Not a Relationship. Does the case involve people who, either by choice or circumstance, need to remain on good terms? Such a case may involve family members, coworkers, a landlord and tenant, neighbors, or others who have a continuing personal or business relationship. One of the advantages of mediation is its ability to resolve a dispute without destroying a relationship.

Filing a lawsuit can be a hostile act. The expressions "to be slapped with a lawsuit" and "hit with a lawsuit" convey the sense of combat and aggressiveness inherent in legal action. Whatever strained relationship two people might have, after legal papers are served it will be worse. Lawyers, motivated by the need to prove the opponent's guilt or liability, will use every means to show that person in the worst possible light.

Indeed, even if the parties want to remain on speaking terms, the lawyers will likely forbid it lest they reveal something to jeopardize their case. In this regard, Professor Jack Ethridge of Emory University Law School observes:

> Litigation paralyzes people. It makes them enemies. It pits them not only against one another, but against the other's employed combatant. Often disputants lose control of the situation, finding themselves virtually powerless. They attach allegiance to their lawyer rather than to the fading recollection of a perhaps once worthwhile relationship.[2]

When the Dispute Is Private, and the Parties Want to Keep It That Way. Nearly everything said or submitted to a court in connection with a lawsuit eventually becomes public record. Only by a special order of a judge can information be sealed, that is, removed from public exposure. Reporters who cover the courts know where to find the information that will make an otherwise boring legal story come alive with interesting personal details. To be sure, open courts are important in a democracy because they give the public a chance to see if prosecutors and judges are doing their jobs well. But from the point of view of individual litigants, public exposure is usually not desired.

Mediation, in contrast, is a strictly private affair. Mediators are bound to protect the confidences entrusted to them during the hearing; there are no stenographers or tape recorders present. In many states, the confidentiality of mediation proceedings is expressly protected by law. Therefore, if parties want to protect confidential business information or just avoid washing their dirty laundry in public, mediation is the forum that provides that privacy.

When the Parties Want to Minimize Costs. Most of the costs in bringing a civil (noncriminal) lawsuit are lawyers' fees. In most major cities today, lawyers' fees range from about $200 to $500 per hour. The median time lawyers spend on a typical civil case, whether in state or federal court, has been found to be about 30.4 hours.[3] At $150 per hour, that comes to more than $4,500.

In contrast, fees for using mediation services range from no charge at nonprofit public mediation centers to $500 or less per party for a half-day session at a typical private mediation service. Although many disputants attend mediation without a lawyer present, even if a lawyer does attend, the party's cost for the lawyer's fee plus the mediation fee, if any, will probably still be much less than if the case had been pursued in court or the lawyer had done all the negotiations from the start.

Former Texas Chief Justice Joseph R. Greenhill observes, "A Chinese proverb says, 'Going to the law is losing a cow for the sake of a cat.' When it costs a cow to gain a cat, mediation is an attractive alternative."[4]

When the Parties Want to Settle a Dispute Promptly. "Our civil courts can be described as parking lots for civil litigation," observed Robert Coulson, former president of the American Arbitration Association (AAA).[5] In some big cities, a litigated case may wait two, three, four, or five years for trial, and though more than 90 percent of cases are settled before trial, settlement discussions often do not get serious until a trial date is near. This aspect of the law has not changed much since 1759, when the British statesman Edmund Burke is said to have observed, "The contending parties find themselves more effectively ruined by the delay than they could have been by the injustice of any decision."

In contrast, at most public mediation centers, mediation sessions are scheduled within a couple of weeks of their submission, and most cases require just one session to reach agreement. Private dispute resolution services take a bit longer because the commercial cases they often handle tend to be more complex. A few months from intake to disposition would be typical.

Factors Opposing Mediation

As valuable a process as mediation can be, there are still times when it may not be in the best interests of one or both of the parties to use it. When disputants want to establish new legal rights, when crimes involving serious bodily injury have occurred, or when a court order is needed immediately to prevent harm—these are circumstances that oppose the use of mediation. At times, indeed, mediation may simply be impossible, as when a party is mentally incompetent.

If any of the following six factors is present in a dispute, mediation is unlikely to be effective and probably should not be used.

When a Party Wants to Prove the Truth or Set a Legal Precedent. Mediation may resolve a dispute, but it is not a way to prove the truth about something. That is because mediated agreements do not establish a right or wrong about what happened in the past; they are concerned only about what will happen in the future. Similarly, there are no "test cases" in mediation. That is, you cannot use mediation to establish a legal precedent because what is agreed between the parties in one dispute does not affect the parties in any other dispute. So if there is a bad law someone wants overturned, or if the person needs to prove the truth of something publicly (for example, a woman who has been defamed in the local paper might want to clear her name), this must be done in court rather than in mediation.

And although it happens rarely, there are disputes in which the facts and the law make it clear that one side is completely right and the other completely wrong, and if taken to court, the completely right side will surely win. A person in such a dispute and on the right side will probably be better off taking her case to court where she will probably win a bigger verdict than she would in mediation, as long as she can tolerate the delays, loss of privacy, and other drawbacks of a lawsuit.

When a Party Wants to Go for the Jackpot. It seems at times to have become an American sport: sue a giant corporation for a huge amount of money, have your lawyer take the case on a contingency fee basis, and hope a sympathetic jury will award you a jackpot.

In point of fact, not as many people win this legal version of the lottery as it may appear. The press plays it up when a jury awards a plaintiff millions of dollars, but often the judge or an appeals court later substantially reduces the award. The reduction seldom gets as much publicity as the original award.

People who want to go for a jackpot against a big company (or even a small company with plenty of insurance) usually choose litigation, not mediation. If they were to mediate such a claim, they might get a settlement more quickly and therefore get their money sooner, but because of the tendency of disputants in mediation to compromise, they would be unlikely to get as much money as if they litigated the claim and carried it all the way to a jury trial. There are no jackpots in mediation. And of course they could also lose in court and recover nothing.

When One Party Is Absent or Incompetent. Mediation normally requires all parties to a dispute to be present for face-to-face discussion. If one or more parties is physically unable to attend, then mediation cannot take place. For example, in a case that once came into my office at a public mediation center, one party to a dispute was eager to mediate, but the other could not attend the session because he was already in jail. More typical is the situation in which one party leaves town. Note, however, that sometimes telephone mediation can work, especially as technology improves for picture teleconferencing. On-line mediation also offers an option for disputants who are not able to meet physically. (For more about on-line mediation, see Chapter Six.)

Mediation also assumes that both parties are rational and can participate in reasoned discussion and negotiation. If one party is mentally impaired or affected by alcohol or drug abuse, mediation will not work.

Physical impairment, however, usually is no bar to mediation. For example, difficulty speaking should not deter anyone from mediation. In one case, an elderly man had great difficulty speaking clearly due to throat surgery, so he brought his lawyer with him to act, literally, as his mouthpiece. Similarly, the fact that someone does not speak English should not be a deterrent. Many public mediation centers have staff who are bilingual in English and Spanish and also keep a roster of mediators who speak other languages.

When One Party Is Unwilling to Mediate. One side to a dispute simply may have no interest in mediating. For example, a man may genuinely prefer litigation because he thinks he has a good chance to win in court; he may not perceive enough of an advantage in mediation to consider trying it; or he may just enjoy the dispute and not be in a hurry to end it.

Nationally, about 30 percent of cases referred to mediation by one party to a dispute or by a neutral party such as a judge or counselor never reach the mediation table because one party declines to participate. Often a mediation service will actively work to bring the reluctant party into mediation, but if that person persists in refusing to participate, the case will not be mediated.

When the Dispute Involves a Serious Crime. Cases involving spouse or child abuse, for example, do not belong in mediation. These are serious crimes and should be prosecuted by the authorities. Mediation requires that both parties be able to engage in rational and effective negotiation. If one party has been the victim of abuse, that party may be too intimidated or fearful of reprisal to participate freely. Also, mediation requires the assistance of a neutral third party. But media-tors are human beings, and faced with evidence of child abuse, for example, few mediators would be able to maintain their neutrality because they would be prejudiced against the abusive party. At many mediation centers, mediators are taught to excuse themselves from cases if they do not feel they could continue in a neutral role.

Other types of major crime, such as those involving serious per-sonal injury or extreme property damage, also do not belong in medi-ation. Minor criminal cases, however, make up a large part of the caseload at many public mediation centers. These are cases involv-ing assault, personal harassment, and minor property damage—cases in which no serious injury or damage has occurred, and the major issue is how much money the offender should pay the victim. These cases usually are referred to the centers by prosecutors before they issue an arrest warrant or by judges who adjourn a court hearing temporarily to see if the parties can reach a settlement.

When One Party Needs a Court Order to Prevent Immediate Harm. A dispute could be a good candidate for mediation except that, by tak-ing the time to mediate, one party might suffer immediate personal or business harm. For example, if town officials announce their intention to cut down all the maple trees lining a residential street by next Thursday, neighbors obviously need to get a judge to issue a court order preventing (enjoining) the town from wielding the ax until the case can be heard. Once they get the court order stopping the tree choppers, the neighbors may want to propose to the judge that the case be put on hold while they and town officials try to resolve it through mediation—but not before.

THE QUESTION OF
TIMING OR "RIPENESS"

In theory, mediation can occur at any point in a dispute. That a court case has been filed, or even that a trial is about to begin, makes no difference. If the parties involved agree, they can always mediate.

As a practical matter, however, the sooner a dispute is brought to mediation the better. Not only can early mediation mean a quick end to uncertainty and anxiety (especially when litigation has begun or is seriously threatened) but it can mean significant savings of money, time, and energy for the parties.

Paradoxically, however, disputes can be brought to mediation *too* early. Indeed, many cases that are suitable for mediation never make it to the table. Or once they do make it, there is no settlement because the parties have jumped the gun and tried to mediate too soon. In the jargon of mediators, these cases are not "ripe." Even people who are big fans of mediation don't like seeing an otherwise mediatable case come to the table too early; if it does, it probably won't settle, and the parties may be turned off to the whole idea of mediation.

So when is a case not ripe for mediation? Here are some examples of cases like that.

If the Parties Have Not Tried to Settle Their Dispute Directly with Each Other. Direct negotiation, as noted earlier, is the most efficient way of resolving any dispute. For example, if you hired a local contractor to put a new roof on your house and came to feel the job was done inadequately, it would make sense for you to call the roofer to try to resolve the problem before calling a mediation service. The understanding each side would get about the other's position (and, indeed, their own position) in direct negotiations would make subsequent mediation much more efficient and likely to succeed.

If Emotions Have Not Had at Least Some Time to Cool. Emotions can run high in many disputes, even those over seemingly mundane matters like putting a new roof on your house. There may be an initial period when one or even both parties are so angry that rational discussion is difficult, if not impossible. It is often best for the parties to cool off a bit before trying to mediate. To continue the earlier example, at the moment your living room ceiling begins to leak because of what you believe was a poor job of reroofing, you may be so angry you'll hardly be able to stand looking at the roofer. In a couple of weeks, however, your emotions may have cooled enough so you can sit down with the roofer in mediation and reasonably consider options for settlement.

If the Parties Don't Have Enough Information About Their Case to Know What They Want to Settle For. Sorting out all the facts that underlie a dispute can take time. In legal terms, the period of investigation is the *discovery*. For example, the victim in an automobile accident would not be ready to mediate until doctors determine whether her injuries will cause a permanent disability. A period of delay would also be advantageous if the parties need to do some legal research or consult a lawyer. Again, with reference to the roofing example, if the dispute concerns reimbursement for water damage to carpets and furniture in the living room, you may need time to get repair and replacement estimates before you can be ready to mediate a settlement.

When It Can Be Too Late to Mediate

Sometimes disputants wait *too* long to mediate. Mediators call these cases "overripe." The usual result of trying to mediate an overripe case is that one side or the other will refuse to participate or, if the mediation occurs, it will fail to produce a settlement. Here are some examples of situations in which it's too late.

If Preparations for Trial Have Proceeded Too Far. Although in theory parties can agree to mediate on the eve of trial, in practice once a party has invested heavily in preparing for trial (that is, has invested in legal fees, time, and effort), she may be much less willing to settle for anything less than what she imagines to be complete victory. By comparison, if mediation is suggested at an earlier stage, parties may be more open to the proposal as a way to avoid the expenses and delays of litigation.

If the People Involved in the Dispute No Longer Control It. This can occur when lawyers become involved who strongly advocate fighting it out in court. In a business situation, it can happen when senior managers or owners take a dispute away from lower-level employees who might have been more likely to settle. I recall one case, for example, involving the buyer for one company and the seller for another; the parties had been doing business together profitably for many years. A dispute arose between them over the quality of goods shipped and, following new procedures set up by one of the companies, the matter was immediately bumped up to senior management. As a result, the people now handling the dispute had had no direct involvement in the underlying transaction. Instead of being motivated to compromise so as to make future business dealings possible, both companies focused on trying to beat the other out of as much money as possible.

If Emotional Links Among the Disputants Are Dead. This happens most often in disputes involving close interpersonal relationships between friends, spouses, and relatives, when hurt feelings have been allowed to fester so long that the parties would rather live with them than risk opening up the entire dispute to try and settle it. For example, a brother and sister fighting bitterly over their mother's estate may be open to trying to resolve the dispute through mediation for a couple of months (or maybe even a year after the mother's death). But if a couple of years pass with grievances still unresolved, the positive feelings they once had for each other may be so dead that neither feels any motivation to resuscitate them through mediation. In short, they would rather stay passively angry than to risk inflaming the old wounds to resolve the underlying dispute.

Timing the Proposal to Mediate

Some cases that are appropriate for mediation don't get to the table, even though they are otherwise ripe, because one side refuses to participate. As we discussed in Chapter One, people may be reluctant to mediate for various reasons: they don't want to invest the time or money; they fear the outcome; or they just don't understand the process and reject it out of ignorance. In my experience, if you have a dispute and want to bring it to mediation, the timing of your proposal to the other side can increase the chances that the other side will agree to participate.

For example, if a lawsuit has been filed, there usually are events—a fact-finding hearing, the pretrial questioning of a physician or other expensive witness, or a court appearance—that promise to be expensive, scary, or have highly uncertain results. A proposal to mediate just before one of these unpleasant events is scheduled to occur may be especially appealing to the other side.

If a case has not yet resulted in a lawsuit, then proposing mediation as a way to avoid legal action can also be appealing. Particularly with interpersonal disputes, a party can make mediation more appealing by proposing it at one of those predictable times during the year when we tend to like to get disputes out of the way. One of these is the end of the year. I've always found, for example, that early December is one of the busiest periods in mediation; people want a clean slate for the new year (and may be motivated by the approaching Christmas season to try to make peace). Therefore, a good time to invite an opponent to mediation would be in the late fall, when the likelihood of having the dispute resolved before the holidays would be an inducement.

Similarly, a proposal to mediate can be effective if made just before some personal event in the other party's life that may put him in a mood to clear the air. Common events likely to trigger such a mood in another person might include an upcoming marriage, birthday, change in employment, anniversary, or birth of a child.

As a mediator, I find it a pleasure to sit at the head of the conference table and be presented with a case in which the subject matter is appropriate for mediation, the parties' interests and needs favor mediation, and the matter is ripe in terms of timing. With such a case, it's likely the mediator, after reasonable effort, will be able to say to the parties, "We have an agreement. Case closed."

THE QUESTION OF POWER IMBALANCE

Sitting down for face-to-face mediation with the contractor who sealed your driveway would not be very intimidating for most people. But what if your opponent was your landlord, or a vice president of the gas and electric company, or even Microsoft? Should you mediate a dispute in which the opponent is far more powerful than you are?

This problem of power imbalance is of concern to mediation professionals, and there are different opinions as to how to handle it. Some advise not attempting mediation with a too-powerful opponent on the theory that it is like taking a lamb to slaughter (with you as the lamb). Others say fears about lambs being slaughtered are greatly exaggerated by opponents of mediation and that mediation has ample protections for the weaker party.

Indeed, significant protections are built into the mediation process. And a person can take other steps to keep from being overwhelmed by a powerful opponent. First, remember that your opponent must have some desire to settle, else she would not take the time to come to mediation. You need to figure out what motivates that desire. Is it the administrative cost of continuing to handle the dispute? Or could it be a concern about bad publicity? Or maybe you have threatened to file a lawsuit (or actually filed one), and your opponent wants to avoid the cost of defending it? If you can understand what motivates your opponent, you can use this understanding to your advantage during negotiations to help even up the balance of power.

Second, checks are built into the mediation system to protect the weaker party. Some mediators take an active, interventionist approach and do their best to ensure that any agreement they oversee is not blatantly unfair—a practice especially common in divorce mediation. Recall too that mediation is voluntary. It is voluntary going in, and it is voluntary going out. If you don't like the way your mediation is shaping up, you can stand up and walk out. If you reach an agreement and then find, when it is ready for signing, that you don't like it, you don't have to sign it. You can also insist that a clause be put in the agreement making it conditional on your lawyer's approval.

A related example of power imbalance occurs when your opponent is someone who, for one reason or another, intimidates you to the point where you cannot effectively represent yourself. There may be some people, such as a former spouse or boss, for example, in whose presence you just feel you cannot speak intelligently, cannot put two thoughts together. In some cases like this, it might be best not to attempt mediation. But again, there are ways to try to make mediation work, even in this situation. You can bring a lawyer or friend to the hearing to help present your case, or, as noted earlier, if you don't like the agreement, you can decline to sign it, or you can make it conditional upon your lawyer's review.

Power imbalance is definitely something to consider in deciding whether to try mediation, but in most cases it should not be decisive because there are enough ways to compensate.

After determining whether a dispute is appropriate and well timed for mediation, the next step is to contact a mediation service and begin the case. In the next chapter, we'll consider the various types of mediation services available and the mediators who work there.

3

Mediators: Who They Are and Where They Work

T he field of mediation, as it has evolved in the United States to date, is vast, disconnected, and unstructured. Mediators work in places as diverse as corporate offices and church basements, court houses and community centers. Often I find that mediators who work in one part of the field have no idea that the rest of the field exists, let alone what mediators do there. It's like the old Indian folk tale of the seven blind men and the elephant: each touches a different part of the animal and draws a different conclusion as to what the beast looks like.

In this chapter, I have divided into six broad categories the most common places where mediators work, the kinds of cases handled there, and the backgrounds of the mediators who work there (see Table 3.1). The categories are (1) community mediation centers, (2) court-connected programs, (3) government programs, (4) private dispute resolution companies, (5) independent mediators in private practice, and (6) corporate, association, and specialty programs. I'll refer to all these as *mediation services*.

With an understanding of these various types of services, you'll have a broad overview of what the mediation field looks like today. Where you might fit in as a mediator will depend on your skills and career goals, as well as the mediation services available in your community.

Table 3.1. Six Types of Mediation Service at a Glance

Mediation Service	Case Types	Mediator Background
Community mediation center	Interpersonal, small claims, landlord-tenant, neighborhood	Varied, no professional background needed
Court-connected program	Contract disputes, personal injuries, divorce, minor criminal complaints	Law, social work, criminal justice, psychology
Government program	Employment discrimination and wrongful termination, taxation, securities	Law, labor relations, securities, human resources
Private dispute resolution companies	Business contracts, personal injuries, construction, employment	Law, business, human resources, accounting, psychology
Independent mediators: Divorce	Divorce and family	Social work, law, psychology, parenting
Independent mediators: Specialty and general	Business, construction, personal injury	Law, business, construction, accounting
Corporate, association, and specialty programs	Employment, real estate, interpersonal, ethnic and religious discrimination	Human resources, social work, business, religious or ethnic background

COMMUNITY MEDIATION CENTERS

Community mediation centers are usually nonprofit organizations that receive funds from state and local governments to provide low-cost mediation services to the public. They are called by various names, such as Dispute Resolution Center, Neighborhood Justice

Center, and Center for Dispute Settlement. In the past twenty-five years, the number of such centers has grown from fewer than a dozen to an estimated five to six hundred from coast to coast; they're in large cities and in small towns. Together the centers handle hundreds of thousands of cases annually.

I'm partial to these centers, having started at one as a volunteer mediator in 1985. From the first day, I was impressed with the skill and dedication of the staff and the remarkably good work they do. For most people thinking of becoming mediators, I recommend these centers as the best place to be trained and then to get some experience handling actual cases to see if you like being a mediator and are any good at it.

In the early years of community mediation, the centers had the reputation of handling mostly what were sometimes irreverently referred to as "park-and-bark" cases—neighborhood disputes involving pets, noise, kids, shared driveways, and the like. I must say, though, there's nothing easy about resolving neighborhood disputes. In my experience, they can be as challenging in their own way as complex, multiparty business cases.

Whether or not park-and-bark was ever a fair description of the early centers' caseloads, today at most centers you're likely to find a mix of neighborhood, consumer, small-business, assault, harassment, victim-offender-reconciliation, and family disputes. The centers' great strength is that they are a cost-effective way of resolving minor cases that often get lost in, or otherwise are not well served by, local courts and the criminal justice system.

Many cases heard at the centers are referred by judges, police, and social service agencies. Examples are charges of assault without injury, personal harassment, and disputes between spouses (see the list in the previous chapter). They also handle disputes brought to them directly by individuals, such as noise from late-night parties, claims of harassment between ex-boyfriends and ex-girlfriends, and consumer small claims such as those involving dry cleaning or auto repair.

Some centers have also developed special programs to meet local needs. For example, centers in college towns may hear many disputes between roommates; centers in rural areas may hear disputes between farmers and feed companies or bankers, or between mobile home park owners and tenants.

Services at public mediation centers are available to all local residents and generally are provided free of charge or at nominal cost (perhaps $10 to $25).

To find out whether there is a center in your community, check the Yellow Pages under "mediation," or try the general information number at City Hall or at the local Bar Association. If this doesn't produce results, check the Web site for the National Association for Community Mediation, an organization that represents more than half the community mediation centers in the country. Their Web site [www.nafcm.org] includes contact information for nearly three hundred centers nationwide. You can also contact the association at 1527 New Hampshire Ave., N.W., Washington, DC 20036; (202) 667-9700.

Who Mediates at Community Mediation Centers?

Most cases at community mediation centers are heard by trained volunteers. Some centers pay mediators a small stipend, maybe $25 or $50 a case. But the bulk of the work is done on a volunteer basis.

These volunteer mediators tend to be people who are good at handling interpersonal disputes, as opposed to complex financial issues, and they bring a diversity of experience to their work. In the state of New York, for example, more than 2,400 citizens over the last twenty years have completed the required twenty-five-hour training program, plus apprenticeship, to serve in the state's network of sixty-two county-based community mediation centers. They come from a variety of professional and work backgrounds: teaching, social work, law, business, parenting and homemaking, and journalism, among others. Most mediators are college-educated, with an average of 3.5 years of mediation experience. Their median age is forty-six.

In Massachusetts, about seven hundred mediators serve at nearly thirty community mediation centers. A statewide study found them to be, on average, "more white, more female, somewhat better off financially, (with) more formal education and somewhat older" than the general population.[1]

Most of the state laws that establish community mediation centers set minimum standards for training. A typical program would involve about twenty-five classroom hours plus a supervised period of apprenticeship.

The following profile is representative of a typical mediator working as a volunteer at a community mediation center. This and all other mediator profiles in this chapter use mediators' real names, are based on interviews, and are used with permission.

MEDIATOR PROFILE

Name: Joan Chisholm

Title: Volunteer mediator

Mediation Service: Community Dispute Settlement Program, Media, Pennsylvania

Educational Background: Master's degree in education with postgraduate work

Years in Practice: 10

Professional Affiliations: African-American Alliance of Peacemakers

Number of Cases Handled in Career: 100s

Current Case Load: 1 or 2 a month (is also a compensated mediator with the U.S. Postal Service)

Case Types: Custody of children of separated and divorced parents; neighborhood disagreements such as shared driveways; disputes with neighbors' children, noise, older neighbors, harassment, and other cases referred by local courts

(Continued)

Most Memorable Mediation Moment: "The parties refused to be in the same room together, so my co-mediator and I had to shuttle back and forth between two rooms. After an hour and a half, the co-mediator convinced them it would be better if they sat down in the same room and faced each other. When they agreed to do that, it felt terrific."

Notable Features of My Conference Room: "I mediate where the parties are—at churches, schools, day care centers."

Philosophy of Mediation: "I try to help people see there is a better path they can take that is nonthreatening and full of promise."

A NOTE ON SMALL CLAIMS COURT

Some consumer claims, neighborhood disputes, and other small cases suitable for mediation at a community mediation center may also be handled in small claims court. Neither forum requires lawyers, and the time it takes to get to small claims court and the token fees involved are about the same as for a community mediation center. So which is the better place to have a case resolved?

Small claims courts are particularly good at handling cases in which the facts and the law are clear and each party's legal rights are plainly spelled out in writing, as in a lease or other contract. Many disputes between landlords and tenants involving nonpayment of rent or return of security deposits, for example, are routinely handled in small claims court. (All small claims courts have limitations on the size of cases they can hear. Upper limits range from about $2,000 to $5,000.)

But small claims judges, like most other judges, have neither the time nor the authority to help disputing parties resolve differences stemming from nonlegal factors such as interpersonal disputes or from complicated fact situations that take a long time to discuss. A judge once explained to me, "Courts are not designed to solve angry feelings. It's like Joe Friday says: 'The facts ma'am, just the facts.'"

Unlike mediation, small claims court offers no privacy from the public or the press. And although it may take only a few weeks to schedule a hearing, you may have to sit in court all morning or all afternoon or all evening waiting for your case to be called. Finally, even if you get a judgment in your favor, there is no guarantee your opponent will actually pay what he owes. In fact, one study has shown that parties in mediation pay what they owe more than twice as often as parties in small claims.[2]

So if a dispute is one that could be heard in small claims, the parties need to weigh these factors in deciding whether small claims or mediation would be most appropriate.

COURT-CONNECTED MEDIATION PROGRAMS

Trial courts in many states have initiated mediation programs as a way to reduce their caseloads and operating costs. Many programs handle civil (noncriminal) cases such as contract disputes and personal injury claims. Other programs handle divorce and family issues, and still others handle minor criminal complaints.

Typically under these programs, before people who file lawsuits are allowed to proceed with their case, they are either required or strongly encouraged to try mediation. States with broad court-referral programs include Florida, Texas, Minnesota, Michigan, California, New Hampshire, Utah, and Georgia, but nearly every state today has some kind of program. A number of other states require that parties receive a written notice about the availability of mediation but do not require them to pursue it.

In some states, the court itself provides the parties with conference rooms and mediators. In others, judges or court clerks simply instruct the parties to pick a mediator from a list of qualified mediators or to go out and find their own mediator.

Who Are the Court-Connected Civil Case Mediators?

Many of the mediators working in court-connected programs mediating contracts, personal injuries, and other civil matters are
lawyers who are paid a stipend for each case. Sometimes they do
this work pro bono, that is, without a fee. These lawyers likely have
had some minimal mediation training, but most do not handle a
high volume of cases; they might mediate just a few cases a year.
In Philadelphia, for example, parties in cases with less than
$50,000 in dispute can use a mediation program run by the local
trial court. All mediators must be lawyers; the court pays the
lawyers $350 per day and provides a brief training session of two to
three hours. Florida courts, however, run an extensive mediation
program for all civil (noncriminal) cases and require substantial
training for their lawyer-mediators.

Other court programs allow parties to choose nonlawyer mediators if they prefer and may provide parties a list of qualified local
mediators, that is, they meet whatever minimal training and experience requirements the court administrators have set.

For a state-by-state summary of court-connected mediation programs, see the Web site of the National Center for State Courts
(www.ncsconline.org) and follow the prompts to "Knowledge Management Offices." Also providing information on court-connected
ADR is the Center for Analysis of Alternative Dispute Resolution
Systems (CAADRS) at their Web address: www.caadrs.org.

Court-Connected Divorce Mediation

Nearly two-thirds of the states have a special type of court-connected mediation to handle divorce cases. Some states simply refer
couples to private mediation services, but in many states (for example, in California), the courts themselves operate extensive mediation programs for divorcing couples. In most of these programs, it is
not the entire divorce that is mediated but the parenting issues such
as child custody and visitation. In a few states, couples can mediate
financial issues such as division of property.

Court-connected divorce mediation is usually provided free or at nominal cost. The mediation is generally of short duration: just one or two sessions is typical. This is because couples usually mediate only the parenting issues and because the volume of cases is high and staff resources are limited.

Mediators in some court-connected programs are required by law to protect the interests of the children—in effect, to act as advocates for the children. As such, a mediator is obligated to raise questions about the children's welfare (even if the child's parents do not) and may block an agreement if it does not protect the children's interests. In a few states, mediators have the power to make a recommendation to the judge if the couple cannot reach an agreement. This power changes the mediator's role from one of neutral facilitator to one of evaluator or arbitrator.

Who Are the Court-Connected Divorce Mediators? When it was new, court-connected divorce mediation often relied on volunteers or part-time court employees as mediators. In recent years, however, these programs have come increasingly to be staffed by full-time, paid employees of the court system who mediate between three and five cases a day.

Many states set stiff qualifications for these full-time mediators that include a minimum educational level or training and experience. Accordingly, these mediators tend to be well educated, often with master's degrees in the social sciences, and professional backgrounds in mental health or family counseling. In Oregon, for example, court-connected mediators must have a master's or law degree, about sixty hours of mediation training, additional course work in areas such as child development, substance abuse, and domestic violence, and two years of work experience in mediation, counseling, or law. Some states still use part-time employees or volunteers as family mediators but do require extensive training and experience.

The following profile is of a mediator who works in court-connected programs and handles both regular civil disputes and custody and other family cases.

MEDIATOR PROFILE

Name: John Polanski

Title: Project Coordinator and Mediator

Mediation Service: Ashtabula County Joint Court Mediation Project, Jefferson, Ohio

Educational Background: Master's in education in community counseling, Youngstown State University, Ohio

Professional Affiliations: Practitioner member and approved consultant, Association for Conflict Resolution

Number of Cases Handled in Career: 450–500

Current Case Load: 10 per week, including custody and visitation, juvenile truancy, contract disputes, and personal injury claims

Most Memorable Mediation Moment: "A divorcing couple in their twenties, whose main focus was, 'I'll get you, you so-and-so,' came in at 4:30 in the afternoon. I decided to challenge them and said, 'I'm willing to stay at the table as long as you are.' They took me up on it and didn't leave my office until 8:30 that night. During those four hours, I watched as they gradually chose to act in favor of their children rather than against each other."

Notable Features of My Conference Room: "Although it's a typical government room with fluorescent lights and white walls, we've made an effort to soften it with plenty of green plants and some art prints."

Favorite Expression Related to Conflict: "There's a better way to do this."

Prosecutor Mediation Programs

Another special type of court-connected program is that run by local public prosecutors or district attorneys. Unlike most court programs that focus on civil disputes, these programs aim to mediate minor criminal complaints.

In Cleveland, for example, the prosecutor's mediation program applies to "nonserious" crimes, such as those involving theft of property valued at less than $300, telephone harassment, and personal menacing without an allegation of use of a weapon or threat of serious bodily harm. Parties bringing such complaints are routinely encouraged to try mediation. The program is voluntary and available at no charge. About three thousand cases are mediated each year. Sessions last about forty-five to sixty minutes. When successful, agreements often call for parties to pay damages, or return property, or avoid contacting each other. Nearly nine of ten cases result in a written settlement with no need for corrective follow-up within the next four weeks—a period the program's directors consider meaningful, given that many of the parties are in ongoing relationships.

Who Are the Prosecutor Program Mediators? Many prosecutor programs are staffed either by full-time court employees with backgrounds in social services or criminal justice, or part-time mediators with legal backgrounds. At some programs, mediations are conducted by law students who are paid a modest stipend for mediating cases during weekend and evening hours.

GOVERNMENT MEDIATION PROGRAMS

Many government departments and agencies have set up mediation programs in recent years as a way to improve services and reduce administrative and litigation costs. At the federal level, for example, the Equal Employment Opportunity Commission (EEOC) uses mediators at regional offices to resolve workplace discrimination claims; the IRS employs mediators to help resolve claims between taxpayers and the agency; and the Farmer-Lender Mediation Program run by the Farmers Home Administration resolves cases between farmers and bankers. The National Association of Securities Dealers (NASD), an independent agency overseen by the U.S. Securities and Exchange Commission (SEC), makes mediators available to people who have disputes with their stock brokers.

These programs are all independent of the Federal Mediation and Conciliation Service (FMCS)—a long-time government agency that mediates contract disputes between employers and unions in the private and government sectors. (For more about the FMCS, the NASD, the EEOC, and other government mediation programs, see Chapter Six.)

Who Are the Government Mediation Program Mediators?

Mediators with federal government programs tend to have backgrounds in law, labor relations, or human relations. Their work generally commands substantial salaries and requires extensive training and experience. Even those who work on contract with government agencies as part-time mediators often have professional backgrounds and advanced degrees.

As an example, see the profile that follows of a mediator with the San Francisco office of the EEOC.

MEDIATOR PROFILE

Name: Mark Keppler

Title: Employment dispute mediator on contract with U.S. EEOC, San Francisco and Los Angeles regional offices

Regular Employment: Director of graduate programs and professor of human resource management at the Craig School of Business, California State University, Fresno

Educational Background: Law degree and master's degree in industrial relations, University of Wisconsin

Years Mediating: 4

Professional Affiliations: Member, Association for Conflict Resolution (merged with Society of Professionals in Dispute Resolution), American Bar Association

Number of Cases Mediated: 100

Current Case Load: 8 per month

Most Memorable Mediation Moment: "In a discrimination case, the employer and employee had reached a tentative agreement after caucusing. I left the employee for two minutes to get the employer's signature. When I returned, she informed me that she had talked to God while I was gone, and He said not to sign the agreement."

Notable Features of My Conference Room: "I generally use government offices. They range in quality from very good to very bad."

Favorite Expression Related to Conflict: "I'm not a judge. I'm a negotiations consultant. I'm here to help you reach your own agreement."

Government agencies that do not employ their own full-time mediators generally provide parties with lists of private mediators who have been screened for education, training, and subject matter knowledge. For example, for its program mediating disputes between stock traders and their brokers, the NASD will refer parties only to outside mediators who have a substantial background in the securities industry as brokers, securities lawyers, or arbitrators.

Many states maintain special offices to monitor and coordinate mediation services throughout the state. Some actually provide services, often for public policy disputes that arise within the state and concern citizen groups and state agencies. But many just act as information clearinghouses. If you want to learn what mediation programs your state operates, the easiest way to find out is probably to contact the statewide mediation or dispute resolution office. A list of statewide offices appears in Resource C.

Private Dispute Resolution Companies

Private dispute resolution is a growth industry. An increasing number of for-profit firms now compete to mediate cases such as contract disputes between businesses, construction cases, employment disputes involving wrongful discrimination and termination, and disputed insurance claims arising out of auto accidents and other mishaps. People and businesses involved in disputes like these—with complex legal and financial issues and substantial amounts of money involved—generally want to use a private firm with experienced, paid mediators rather than a community mediation center with volunteer mediators.

The primary functions of a private dispute resolution company are to

- Provide a panel of trained and experienced mediators

- Get all parties to agree to participate in mediation

- Administer the mediation, including all paperwork, scheduling, and billing

- Follow up with the parties after mediation if further dispute resolution services are needed

There are hundreds of private dispute resolution firms. Some operate at the national level, with offices in major cities; others are mid-size or small firms that operate regionally or locally.

The biggest national firm is JAMS (the name formerly stood for Judicial Arbitration & Mediation Services), which is headquartered in Irvine, California. This company has about twenty offices nation-wide and generates some $55 million in annual sales. Other national firms include Resolute Systems, Inc., headquartered in Milwaukee, Wisconsin, and National Arbitration & Mediation, Inc., in Great Neck, New York. The American Arbitration Association, Inc., in New York City and Arbitration Forums, Inc., in Tampa, Florida, are well-established nonprofit corporations that handle many of the same kinds of large, complex disputes as the for-profit companies.

Fees at most of the private firms generally start at a minimum of about $500 per party for a half-day mediation session. Costs can rise to thousands of dollars, depending on the complexity of the case and the length of time needed to resolve it. (For a list of some of the larger national and regional private dispute resolution firms, see Resource D.)

Who Are the Private Dispute Firm Mediators? Most of the larger private firms and many of the smaller ones maintain a list of people available to mediate disputes. The lists are usually referred to as *mediation panels*. The panel is a list or roster of mediators available through that firm. Most panel members are former judges and practicing attorneys; others may have expertise in subjects such as engineering, health care, construction, and land use. Panel members are usually not employees of the company but work as independent contractors, although owners of smaller mediation firms may themselves be mediators who are available to handle cases. For example, two or three mediators may have gotten together to form a local dispute resolution company. They run the business, mediate some of the cases, and assign the rest to members of their panel of outside mediators. The bigger companies' panels sometimes include "career mediators" who have advanced mediation training and experience and who mediate full-time, often with a specialty such as construction, business, or employment disputes.

Some popular members of a company's panel may be selected to mediate weekly or a couple times a month; others may be selected just a few times a year. Mediators may be exclusive to one company, or they may appear on the panels of several companies. It all depends on how much they are in demand and whether any particular company is able to generate enough business to sign up mediators to work with that company exclusively. For example, all the retired judges on panels maintained by California-based JAMS work only for that firm. If a person wants one of these judges to mediate her case, she'll have to go to JAMS. But a lawyer with mediation training in a mid-size city may appear on the panels of several local or regional companies, none of which keeps her busy enough to use her services exclusively.

Companies may have just one panel of mediators, or they may have several panels organized by the subject area of the mediators' specialty. For example, a company active in a number of different types of mediation may have a Negligence Panel composed of lawyers and judges familiar with accident claims; a Health Care Panel composed of health care lawyers, physicians, and hospital administrators; and a Construction Panel composed of construction lawyers, engineers, architects, builders, and contractors of various specialties.

Private firms can differ hugely in terms of how much training and skill their mediators have. At one extreme, they often provide the most highly skilled career mediators. Yet paradoxically, it is also on these firms' panels where you are likely to find inexperienced mediators. This often results from the firms' habit of hiring big-name judges who have recently retired. Judges with little background or training in mediation may believe their role is just to "knock people's heads together" until they settle, as they did when they were on the bench. Similarly, a private firm's panel may include a lawyer-mediator with great specialized knowledge and reputation in a particular area of the law but who is largely untrained and inexperienced in mediation.

Following are profiles of two retired judges—both well trained and experienced—who mediate with private firms. I include profiles of two judges rather than one because each has insightful comments to share that could only come from real-life experience at the head of the mediation table.

MEDIATOR PROFILE

Name: Hon. Anton J. Valukas

Title: Mediator-arbitrator on contract with Resolute Systems, Inc., Chicago

Regular Employment: Retired supervising judge, Pre-Trial Mediation Division, Circuit Court of Cook County, Chicago

Educational Background: Law degree, DePaul College of Law; L.L.B., J.D., Chicago

Years Mediating with Private Firm: 6

Number of Cases Handled: 300–400

Current Case Load: 4 to 5 per month, including malpractice, personal injury, contracts, and general civil matters

Most Memorable Mediation Moment: "A ten-year-old boy was hit by a truck and left a paraplegic. Four years later, the parties came to mediation. They later told me they had never intended to settle. But after six hours they reached an agreement. The boy was present. Though he had difficulty holding up his head, when we settled he grasped my hand, gave me a smile, and said 'Thanks.'"

Favorite Expression Related to Conflict: "In all my cases, I sit the parties down, get acquainted, and say, 'There are three things I can assure you of: (1) I am neutral and this playing field is as level as this table; (2) I will never violate a confidence or a trust; and (3) I'll never tell you my age.' That relaxes them."

MEDIATOR PROFILE

Name: Hon. Leon A. Beerman

Title: Mediator, National Arbitration & Mediation, Inc., New York City

Regular Employment: Retired judge, New York State Supreme Court, Queens County (for twenty years)

Educational Background: Law degree, New York University, 1941

Years Practicing as Mediator: 4

Number of Cases Handled in Career: 400

Current Case Load: 10 cases per week, mostly personal injury claims

Most Memorable Mediation Moment: "I had a case where a man had apparently injured his wrist in a car accident and was claiming permanent disability. I asked him, 'What is it you cannot do now that you could do before?' He says, 'In church on Sundays, when they come to Hallelujah!, I can't clap.'"

Notable Features of My Conference Room: "I have an American flag on display behind me where I sit at the head of the table, just to provide a symbol of justice."

Philosophy of Mediation: "It's a way to do justice, or at least substantial justice, so that nobody gets hurt and both parties know the matter has been resolved."

INDEPENDENT MEDIATORS IN PRIVATE PRACTICE

Independent mediators in private practice generally work on their own, unaffiliated with private dispute resolution companies or other mediation services. It can be economical for disputants to use an independent mediator when they don't need or want to pay for the help of a private dispute resolution company. Perhaps all parties readily agree to mediate and are able to arrange the session themselves. The cases independent mediators usually handle—those involving substantial money, property, or legal rights—typically are not heard at community mediation centers.

Whether they practice locally or nationally, independent mediators set their own fees, handle their own paperwork, keep their own schedules, and often develop and use their own rules. Fees range from $100 to $300 an hour for independent mediators who work at the local level and handle a general variety of cases, to $1,000 to $5,000 a day for full-time mediators who operate nationally and specialize in large, complex disputes in areas such as business and construction.

Independent mediators have practices that generally fall into one of three categories: (1) divorce and family mediators, (2) specialty mediators, and (3) general mediators. We'll consider each of these next.

Divorce and Family Mediators

Most people who make any kind of a full- or part-time living as an independent mediator do so by handling divorce cases. Divorce mediation is probably the most well-established part of mediation practice; in many large and medium-size cities, upwards of 25 percent of divorcing couples go through mediation.

Most divorce mediators practice by themselves or sometimes as part of a small group. Divorce mediation lends itself to independent practice because a sole practitioner can build a practice by contacting through mail, phone calls, and personal visits the major sources of case referrals in her community, such as therapists, clergy, and divorce lawyers. And the mediator can charge enough ($125 per hour is typical in a mid-size city) to make a living.

Unlike court-connected divorce mediation, in which program administrators assign a mediator to work with a couple, in private mediation couples voluntarily retain the services of a mediator of their own choosing. The couple can choose to make their mediation comprehensive and cover all the issues in their divorce, including parenting and financial issues, or to limit it to certain issues, usually custody and visitation. A half-dozen or more sessions may be required, depending on the number and complexity of issues addressed.

Most divorce mediators advise both spouses, particularly when substantial assets are involved, to consult with their own lawyers during the mediation process in order to understand their legal rights and the range of settlement options that would likely be approved by a local court. The lawyers do not attend the sessions with the spouses or actively represent them; rather, the spouses use the lawyers as informational resources. At the conclusion of the mediation, the mediator prepares a Memorandum of Understanding for the couple. This document, written in understandable English rather than legalese, sets out all of what the couple agreed to concerning money, property, children, and other issues. Later, perhaps after another round of lawyer review, the terms of the memorandum are incorporated into the official divorce decree.

The skills mediators develop in working with divorcing couples translate well to other interpersonal disputes, such as those involving family members, friends, and coworkers; and many divorce mediators like to round out their practice with such cases.

Who Are the Divorce Mediators? In theory, anyone can hang out a shingle and declare herself to be a divorce mediator. Most divorce mediators who are serious about their practice, however, first take a standard forty-hour training course with a trainer approved by the Association for Conflict Resolution (ACR)—a national, merged organization that includes what formerly had been the Academy of Family Mediators—then affiliate with ACR in order to continue their education and keep current on new developments in the field. (For more information on becoming trained to be a divorce mediator, see Chapter Five.)

Some time ago, the former Academy of Family Mediators (before it merged into ACR) did a survey of its membership and found that, of nearly two thousand active members,

• Forty percent have a background in law, 30 percent in therapy or social work.

- Eighty percent hold a master's degree, a Ph.D., or law degree.

- Seventy percent are between the ages of forty and fifty-nine.

- Sixty percent are female.

- Seventy percent are in solo practice.

MEDIATOR PROFILE

Name: Dolly Hinckley

Title: Divorce and family mediator

Mediation Service: Self-employed, doing business as Divorce Mediation Associates in Rochester, New York

Educational Background: B.S. in business administration (management), University of Buffalo, Buffalo, New York

Professional Affiliations: Practitioner member and approved consultant, ACR; board of directors, New York State Council on Divorce Mediation

Number of Cases Handled in Career: 800–900

Current Case Load: 15

Most Memorable Mediation Moment: "A bright, middle-aged couple with two children, ages three and ten, bickered intensively during five months of divorce mediation. At the last session, after concluding an agreement and committing to work cooperatively in the future to parent their children, in my presence—spontaneously and triumphantly—they hugged each other."

Notable Features of My Conference Room: "I use a large, comfortable room in my home decorated with items from my travels around the world, including two, thirty-inch-tall African fertility statues."

Favorite Expression Related to Conflict: "Conflict is inevitable, but fighting is a choice."

Specialty Mediators

Some highly skilled and entrepreneurial-minded mediators make a good living specializing in large, complex cases, such as those involving business ownership and employee relations, construction, patents and copyrights, environment, land use, or other matters of public policy.

Many of these full-time, specialty mediators travel extensively, hearing cases throughout their region or around the country. One mediator, for example, a national specialist in construction cases, has mediated disputes between owners and builders of shopping centers, sports stadiums, and college dormitories, often with six or seven parties involved. Over the years, he has worked with leaders in the construction field—lawyers, developers, engineers, and architects—and so has developed a reputation and clientele that keep him jetting around the country as he is called on to mediate cases for up to $3,000 a day.

Not all specialty mediators have quite this busy and lucrative a career; some do well conducting their practice in just one large city or region. Still, to be successful in this way requires good mediation skills and strong entreprenuerial drive. We'll talk more about what it takes to develop a full-time practice as a specialty mediator in Chapter Six.

MEDIATOR PROFILE

Name: Joseph Grynbaum

Title: Construction mediator

Mediation Service: Self-employed, doing business as "Mediation Resolution International," based in West Hartford, Connecticut; publishes e-mail newsletter on developments in the construction industry.

Educational Background: B.S. in mechanical engineering, Caulfield Institute of Technology, Melbourne, Australia

Years in Practice as Mediator: 3

Professional Affiliations: Member, ACR; associate member, Section on Dispute Resolution, American Bar Association

Number of Cases Handled in Career: 6

Current Case Load: 2

Most Memorable Mediation Moment: After a successful mediation, the lawyer for one side said, "Going into this mediation after three years of belligerent litigation, I could never imagine we'd settle."

Notable Feature of My Mediation Sessions: I have a "no buts" rule. I ban the word *but* because it dilutes the positive aspect of a statement made to the opposite side. The rule also gives everyone a shared role in controlling each other's slippages during the session.

Favorite Expression Related to Conflict: "An ounce of mediation is worth a pound of arbitration and a ton of litigation."

General Mediators

A small but growing number of mediators now earn their living by conducting a general mediation practice, taking a variety of business and legal disputes—essentially, whatever comes through the door. Until recently, this kind of practice was rare because there just was not enough business to keep a general mediator busy. Fortunately, as mediation has continued to grow in popularity, a modest but increasing number of mediators are now able to conduct a general practice. (For more on establishing and running a general mediation practice, see Chapter Six.)

A Note on Part-Time Mediation

Some independent mediators work only part-time; for their primary income, they rely on some other profession or occupation such as law, business, or social work. Part-time mediators may be listed on the panels of private dispute resolution companies. Or they may be called to mediate through court-connected or government agency programs or through programs run by professional associations to which they belong.

Some part-time mediators are well trained and highly skilled, but some don't take mediation seriously, have received little or no training, and view part-time mediation either as an easy way to pick up extra cash or to add some class to their resume. A news magazine once referred to this group as, "Have Business Card, Will Mediate."

There's nothing wrong with being actively engaged in another line of work and mediating on the side. If you choose to take that route, however, I urge you to be serious about getting quality training and enough experience so that when you do have the opportunity to sit at the head of the table as a mediator—even if it's just on occasion—the people seated to your right and your left receive competent, professional services.

Corporate, Association, and Specialty Mediation Programs

These mediation services include programs run by large businesses, professional associations, and distinct population groups. These services don't generally employ large numbers of mediators, but they can offer interesting challenges to mediators who happen to have a connection with the sponsoring organization.

Corporate In-House Mediation Programs

Many large businesses, seeking new ways to improve productivity and worker satisfaction, have discovered the value of in-house dispute resolution programs to improve communication among staff, resolve conflicts, and reduce the likelihood of violence in the workplace. Typically, selected staff members (managers and employees of different ages, ethnic backgrounds, and job descriptions) are trained to act as mediators. Then when disputes arise between or among employees, the disputants are invited (or sometimes required) to go to mediation conducted by one of the staff mediators. For example, Bally's, a Las Vegas resort with four thousand employees, established an in-house mediation program. Twenty-four staff members, representing a wide cross-section of employees from senior management to support staff and including union members, were trained by mediators from the local community mediation center. Their training included techniques for handling employee disputes, interdepartmental conflicts, and supervisor-employee disputes. A company spokeswoman said the program had the added benefit of reducing management time spent dealing with internal company conflicts.

To find out if the corporation you work for has an in-house mediation program, inquire with the human resources office or Office of General Counsel.

Associations' Mediation Programs

As professional associations and other membership groups seek new ways to serve their members, many have established mediation programs. For example, the National Association of Realtors began the Home Buyer/Home Seller Dispute Resolution Program to help mediate claims by home buyers or sellers against real estate agents. Similarly, the National Association of Electrical Engineers started a program to help resolve claims against its members. These and similar programs often train current or retired members of the associations to act as mediators. To see if an association to which you have a connection has a mediation program, check the group's Web site or contact the national office. Many such groups are headquartered in Washington, D.C., New York City, or other large cities.

Specialized Mediation Services

As mediation gains in popularity, some specialized groups, including business trade organizations and religious groups, have begun to develop their own networks of mediation services. The following are a few of the specialized programs available.

Peacemaker Ministries. This national group, with a network of trained conciliators around the country, uses Christian biblical principles of conflict resolution to mediate disputes. The organization trains and certifies its own conciliators; the group includes people from many professional and work backgrounds: lawyers, mental health counselors, clergy, homemakers, and business people. For information, contact Peacemaker Ministries, 1537 Avenue D, Suite 352, Billings, MT 59102; (406) 256-1583, or visit their Web site: www.HISPEACE.org.

Lesbian and Gay Community Services Center: Center Mediation Services/Project Resolve. This program helps lesbian, gay, bisexual, transgender, and people with HIV-AIDS and their families to resolve conflicts outside the court system. Matters commonly addressed include relationship breakups, child custody and visitation issues, and disputes within and among community groups. Mediators include lawyers, mental health professionals, teachers, activists, and health care workers. All services are free of charge. The group operates in the New York City area and can provide referrals to similar services nationally. For more information, contact Center Mediation Services/Project Resolve at 208 West 13th St., New York, NY 10011; (212) 620-7310, or visit their Web site: www.gaycenter.org.

Asian Pacific American Dispute Resolution Center. This organization provides mediation and conciliation services in Asian Pacific languages, including Chinese, Korean, Japanese, Vietnamese and, Tagalog (Philippines). The center handles ethnic disputes, as well as domestic, housing, neighborhood, employment, and business conflicts, and matters involving race relations. Disputants are asked to pay nominal processing and hourly fees, but fees are waived for those unable to pay. The center primarily serves Los Angeles County but assists those outside the area by conducting telephone mediation and by making referrals nationally to mediators or translators fluent in Asian Pacific languages. For information, contact the Center at 1145 Wilshire Blvd., Suite 100, Los Angeles, CA 90017; (213) 250-8190, or visit their Web site: apadrc.apanet.org.

As we've seen, there are many different types of mediation services. This overview has been designed to help you understand how the field is organized and where you might fit in. In the next chapters, we'll consider what it takes to become a mediator and how to get trained.

4

Personality Traits of
Successful Mediators

Over the years, I've found that as many as three-fourths of people who pay for and complete mediator training—a course of study that usually involves twenty-five to forty hours in the classroom—never actually practice as mediators. I think what happens is they belatedly discover they are not suited to the work. Some find they are simply not good at mediating; others can mediate well but don't really enjoy it.

I noticed this phenomenon as far back as when I took my first mediator training in 1985 at a public mediation center in Rochester, New York. There were about thirty-five other people in the class. I'm unsure how many of those were mediating two or three years later, but I doubt if it was more than a handful.

Today I see a similar situation. For example, there's a successful divorce mediator in our community—I'll call him Frank—who supplements his client fees by training a couple dozen people every year to become divorce mediators. Frank's friends scratch their heads and ask, "Isn't Frank just creating his own competition?" But Frank knows the same thing I realized long ago: of all those who take mediation training, relatively few will actually end up practicing.

I noted earlier that in most cases one needs no particular background to become a mediator; for the most part, the field remains

open to all. Accordingly, whether you choose to become a mediator depends initially on your own assessment of whether you are
suited to the role.

There's no point in investing your time and money in getting
trained, only to find you're not suited to the work. So in order to
help you think about whether becoming a mediator is right for you,
we'll consider which motivations for wanting to be a mediator make
sense and which do not, and what skills and personality traits successful mediators tend to have in common.

Interestingly, I have been unable to find even one article in professional mediation journals on the question of what type of personality good mediators have. The reason may be that the question
leans toward the politically incorrect, and also simply because it's
so tricky. I'm sure I could list ten personality traits needed to be a
successful mediator and then discover people who lack all of these
but have other qualities that make them good mediators. Nevertheless, I think it's helpful to consider these predilections before
you make the decision to enter the profession. Recognizing that
this is at best only a rough answer to a tough question, I share some
thoughts on the personal qualities that tend to make someone a
successful mediator.[1]

THE MOTIVATION TO MEDIATE

People have many different reasons for wanting to become a
mediator. Some of these are based on a practical understanding
of the field, but others may be based more on wishful thinking
than reality. How do the various motivations tend to play out
once people begin practicing? Let's consider five reasons people
often have for entering this field; two of them I think are good
reasons and will lead to a satisfying career; the other three, I fear,
will tend to produce a dissatisfied and perhaps not very successful mediator.

GOOD REASONS TO
BECOME A MEDIATOR

Many people who have become mediators and found satisfying careers did so for one or more of the three reasons discussed in the sections to follow.

To Be of Service

Ours has been called a litigious society. We have more than a million lawyers and file more lawsuits per person than any other nation in the world. To the slightest point of conflict, our conditioned battle cry is, "See you in court!" As one observer noted, "We call our lawyers to sue before we call our opponents to talk." Some of the lawsuits people bring might be amusing if they weren't so pathetic: the group of parents who sued all the way to federal court over an official's error in a high school football game; the man who sued a restaurant because his pat of butter weighed less than two full ounces.

Although mediation is not a cure-all, it can help resolve perhaps a majority of our interpersonal disputes and a large portion of other types of disputes without litigation, saving people from wasting time and money, freeing them from lawyers, and helping them solve their problems without destroying their important personal, family, and business relationships.

We need more people to help transform our society from one of aggressive conflict to one of cooperative problem solving. We need those who can help people work out solutions to their own problems quickly, fairly, and inexpensively so they can get on with their lives. To be a part of this historic transformation is a worthy reason to become a mediator and a motivation that will sustain you through both the uplifting and the frustrating parts of the work.

As mediator and trainer Jim Melamed observes: "There's a significant number of our mediators who enjoy and are attracted to mediation as a way of being of service—and they really are of service to their communities. I say to these mediators, 'As mediators you are doing God's work. You are on the front lines beating swords into plowshares and helping people do it for themselves'" (personal communication; see Note 1).

Enjoyment of the Process

Mediation is a unique enterprise in the sense that mediators get an intimate view into people's lives—"a full-breadth window on the human condition" is how Jim Melamed puts it. If you're mediating a divorce, or a business case with underlying personnel issues, or even a personal injury matter in which a person's ability to navigate life is in question, it can be both stimulating and profoundly satisfying to be involved so closely with real people and their problems. Many find they enjoy this close-up view of others' lives and challenges and find great satisfaction in learning how people function and how they can be supported in solving their problems.

For me, there are few pleasures as gratifying as meeting two disputants in my office at nine o'clock in the morning and by midafternoon watching them shake hands and leave with a signed agreement. A recent case involved a father and twenty-seven-year-old son who had been estranged for many years. The son said the father cared little for him and was too busy for him. The father said it was impossible to talk with his son because he would blow up at the most innocent remark. We met for four hours over two lateafternoon sessions. They worked hard, owned up to their parts in the dispute, and reached deeply to find solutions. At the end of the second session, they worked together to come up with the terms of an agreement: regular family dinners, weekly meetings for coffee, use of civil language, respect for each other's work, and so on. I read the agreement aloud; they signed it, then I signed it. As they put on their coats to leave, the son turned to his father and said, "I really do love you, Dad," and the father said, "I love you, too, son." They embraced, and left together. It was their effort, much more than mine, that yielded the good result, but after they closed the door and I was alone, I thought how thankful I am for the opportunity to do this kind of work.

Not all cases end so well, of course. Some sputter along, accomplishing little; some end without an agreement. But even in these, one can enjoy working with people as they try hard to resolve difficult problems. Even if it's just one of them working hard, or even if its just one of them part of the time working hard, there can still be pleasure in it for the mediator. Even when it's frustrating it can be fascinating.

Making a Good Living

If you think you can derive this kind of enjoyment from helping move people, with care and respect, through the mediation process—whatever the results—you have a good reason to become a mediator.

Is a desire to make a lot of money a good reason to become a mediator? I don't think so. In fact, the urge to get rich is number two on my list of reasons *not* to become a mediator, which I'll get to later. Nevertheless, I strongly believe that if you enter this field for the right reasons—the desire to serve and because you enjoy the work—you should be able to make a decent living.

As an inspirational example, I offer the experience of my friend Esther, who practiced law for about fifteen years and came to hate it. At around age forty, she quit the law firm and decided to become a divorce mediator. She took first-rate mediation training, rented a small office in a Victorian house on a side street just outside downtown, and opened her practice. During the course of the first year, Esther sent letters of introduction to nearly every therapist in town, every member of the clergy, and every divorce lawyer. She followed up with telephone calls, met with many of these people, and took a lot of them to lunch. Before long, she had a steady flow of clients and gradually raised her rate to $150 an hour—the top rate for divorce mediators where I live.

Between sessions with clients and out-of-session (unbilled) time reviewing paperwork and drafting agreements, Esther bills about thirty hours a week. She still works out of the same small office and has only one part-time secretary. Esther's now in her tenth year of practice. She's become so busy that people have to wait for an appointment. If you and your spouse have the misfortune to need her services, the earliest she can see you is about twelve weeks from now.

Not all mediators do as well financially as Esther, not by a long shot. In fact, she's at the high end of what private practitioners tend to make. Still, people do make a living at mediation. Some do it the way Esther did—by building a successful solo practice. Some do it in a group practice; others do it by being employed full-time with the courts or a government agency or a large business corporation.

This wasn't always the case. Ten or twenty years ago, about the only people making a living at mediation were a few hot-shot business mediators flying around the country resolving multi-million-dollar construction disputes. But that has changed: mediation is more accepted; it is even sought-after today. Now there are Esthers in most large cities making a pretty good living on divorce cases. Others are doing well with civil disputes, business cases, and environmental matters. Still others teach and train or work in human resource offices of large corporations. Add to that another set of jobs in what I call *mediation support:* people who administer private dispute resolution companies or government programs, those who sell the services of private firms, those who operate Internet mediation services, and those who teach conflict resolution in the schools or train other mediators.

If your motivation is right—you have the desire to serve and love the process of mediation—I believe your own energy and enjoyment of the work will lead you to a satisfying and remunerative career. In Chapters Six and Seven, we'll talk more about where the jobs are and how much they pay.

REASONS NOT TO BECOME A MEDIATOR

Some of the reasons people often give for wanting to become mediators are not necessarily good or helpful. If you enter the field for one or more of these reasons, you run a good chance of becoming frustrated by the experience.

To Promote a Cause

Some people go into mediation thinking it will give them a forum within which to promote a cause or mission. A man who has been through a bitter divorce, for example, may decide to become a divorce mediator with the attitude that "I'm not going to let another father go through what I went through." Or a woman might want to enter the field to promote women's rights, or someone else may want to advocate for the rights of disabled people, or minorities, or the environment.

There are many legitimate and righteous causes, but mediation is not the way to promote them. Not only would advocating for one's personal interests during mediation violate the mediator's ethical requirement to be neutral (see Resource B for more discussion) but the parties would become suspicious, if not paranoid, about a mediator with a personal agenda. Indeed, a necessary trait of a good mediator is the ability to control one's own bias and to be respectful and sensitive to the parties' strongly felt values, including gender, ethnic, cultural, and political differences. In short, a mediator with a cause violates professional ethics and quickly becomes an ineffective mediator.

To Get Rich

I mentioned earlier that it's fine to become a mediator in order to earn a good living, but it's also true that few mediators actually get rich. As noted, most mediators charge by the hour, and few people other than corporate lawyers get rich charging by the hour. At $100 to $150 an hour you can earn a good living, but you aren't going to become wealthy; there are just not enough hours in a day. As Jim Melamed puts it, "People who come into the field intending to get rich will likely end up in other places because there is not a whole lot of blue sky; you're basically grinding the work out."

And don't think you'll get wealthy mediating huge, multi-million-dollar business disputes because it's against mediator ethics to charge based on the outcome of a case (see Resource B). You can't charge, say, 1 percent of the amount of the settlement; you have to charge your regular hourly fee.

The only person I know who really made a killing in mediation (or seems to have done so; one never really knows) is a fellow who started a private dispute resolution company and then, just as the stock market was booming, offered shares to the public. On the day after the stock offering, he was $4 million richer than he had been the day before. Exactly how much of that money found its way into his pocket and how much he had to use to keep the company afloat (the company lost money most years), I'm not sure.

In sum, my message it this: if you're thinking of becoming a mediator to become wealthy, you're likely to be disappointed.

To Solve Other People's Problems

Some people like to solve other people's problems. You probably know the type. At the office they are always willing to close the door and listen to someone else's personal or business dilemma. But they don't stop with just listening; they go the next step and tell the troubled person exactly what to do and how to do it. Sometimes they want a full report later about how their advice worked out. It's good to have people like this around. The only problem is, except for the listening part, it's not what mediators do.

Good mediators overcome the temptation to solve the parties' problem and instead are content to support the parties' efforts to solve their problem themselves. More often than not, people who become mediators because they like to solve others' problems are surprised when they see how resistant the parties' are when they try to impose their own solutions.

Similarly, some people are drawn to mediation for the challenge of getting disputants to make an agreement. We see this most often with other professionals—notably lawyers—who are used to achieving positive outcomes for their clients. They just love the challenge of charging right into a conflict and getting results! But sometimes the more the mediator emphasizes results, the more resistant the parties become. Seasoned mediators know that often it's only by letting go of concern for results that they can get a good result. It's a paradox, but true. Sometimes it's only when the mediator can say, "Folks, it's really OK with me if you choose not to reach an agreement," that the parties become willing to take ownership of the dispute and get serious about settling.

So if you're thinking of becoming a mediator so you can tell everyone else how to solve their problems or because you love the challenge of getting results, think again.

AT A GLANCE
THE MOTIVATION TO MEDIATE

Good Reasons to Become a Mediator

- To Be of Service

- To Enjoy the Process

Reasons Not *to Become a Mediator*

- To Promote a Cause

- To Get Rich

- To Solve Other People's Problems

CAUTION: MEDIATING CAN BE LONELY, STRESSFUL, AND EMOTIONALLY DRAINING

I've heard many people say over the years how much they would prefer mediating to putting up with the stress of law practice, business, academia—whatever it is they're currently doing. I have to believe they've given little thought to what mediators really do.

It can, of course, be a tremendous ego trip to sit down with people and help them work out their problems. It can be uplifting, a natural high, a great source of satisfaction. You can go home at the end of the day feeling you've really accomplished something. But mediators pay a price. Labor mediator and professor Jerome T. Barrett, in his paper "The Psychology of a Mediator," identifies aspects of mediating that can exact a psychic cost:[2]

ISOLATION: most of the mediator's work is done in isolation from colleagues and supervisors.

HELPER ROLE: the mediator's power is limited to that of a helper; without the will of the disputing parties, the mediator is powerless to make things happen.

LIMITED POSITIVE FEEDBACK: the very human needs of the mediator for recognition, appreciation, and respect are generally unfulfilled by the parties, as they focus on their own disputes.

CONFIDENTIAL INFORMATION: the absolute requirement of confidentiality places on the mediator the same pressures that a priest has regarding confession and a lawyer has with a client.

FILTERED REACTION ROLE: to maintain their impartial role and retain their effectiveness, mediators must suppress such normal reactions as frustration, hostility, and anger and replace them by neutral or opposite reactions.

In summary, observes Barrett,

> [the mediator is] an outside intervenor, working under high stress on the problems of others . . . in isolation from any support groups, and bound by a strict code of confidentiality. The mediator's opportunities for positive feedback are limited, the success of his performance is difficult to measure, and he is subjected to the manipulations of the parties.

Yet "in spite of the psychic costs," concludes Barrett, "there is no shortage of candidates for the job, and incumbents talk glowingly about a 'high' from achieving a difficult settlement."

My advice is still this: you should enter this field with your eyes open.

DESIRED SKILLS AND PERSONALITY TRAITS

Assuming one enters the field for the right reasons, are there particular skills or personality traits likely to make one a successful mediator? I think most mediators would agree, based on their experience and observations, that some skills and traits are common among those who succeed in this field. The skills can often be learned, but the traits are more often innate.

Nevertheless, most mediators would acknowledge that someone with very different skills and traits could also make a good mediator. Michael Lang, a seasoned mediator and trainer, expressed this well when I asked him about mediator personalities. He wrote:

> I am asked this question often in trainings, particularly because many of the participants experience me as having a personality that is well-suited to the work (calm, able to tolerate ambiguity, respectful, empowering, etc.). At the same time, I know many mediators whose personalities differ vastly from mine and whom I regard as superior mediators.[3]

So with that disclaimer, I offer, as generalizations only, the following guidelines that may help you assess your suitability for the field.

Good Listening Skills

We spoke in Chapter One about the crucial role listening skills play in the mediator's ability to understand what a dispute is about and to earn the participants' trust. We labeled this kind of listening *empathic*, as it involves listening not only to the facts but to the parties' emotional reactions to them. "Once participants have had the experience of being heard fully by the mediator," observes Jim Melamed, "they are willing to turn over leadership of the mediation to the mediator; but before they have had that experience, they will resist the mediator's lead."

Mediator training devotes a great deal of time to the theory of good listening, as well as to role plays to practice specific techniques. So although good listening skills come naturally to some people, for others it is a skill that can be developed.

Ability to "Read" People

When we're mediating, parties give us information about the dispute during their opening statements, in joint discussions, and even more in private caucus. Even so, the parties seldom tell us everything we need to know about the dispute, their reactions to it, and their willingness to consider various options for settlement. Indeed, throughout the session, unexpressed interests, needs, and emotions float about the room. Therefore, the ability to read the parties—a largely intuitive ability to sense the things we are not being told, to perceive emotions that linger just below the surface and to push with questions a bit further in a particular direction—can go a long way toward making one successful as a mediator.

Melamed suggests that an ability to read people is often a function of a mediator's own psychological make-up, specifically the tendency to have a high need for approval—a need often unmet, as I've noted, due to the limited positive feedback available to most mediators. Nevertheless, notes Melamed,

> I believe people who have a high "need for approval"
> make good mediators because they develop the tendency
> of always looking around to make sure others are happy
> and satisfied. Those same abilities—to notice subtle cues

of acceptability or resistance—make all the difference in the world because the mediator is always primed to "read" the participants' earliest possible indication of their potential attraction or resistance to various settlement options. For example, a mediator with this skill will pick up the parties' earliest nonverbal indicators of assent, not by staring at them but by perceiving cues in his peripheral vision. With this ability, the mediator can maneuver the discussion toward the desired terms of settlement.

An intuitive ability seems to be innate in some people; others seem to develop it as they go through life. Unlike good listening skills, however, I do not think much of it can be taught.

Facility with Language

Like psychological counseling and therapy, mediation is a "talking cure." The entire process, from opening statements on, involves words. Accordingly, a facility—indeed, a precision—with language seems essential to successful mediation. Mediators who fire off words casually, like cannon shot, may quickly find themselves in trouble, perhaps having said things that weren't as clear or as neutral, respectful, or caring as they should have been. Throughout the session, the mediator must repeatedly and sometimes quickly capture and echo back in a few precise words the sometimes puzzling stories and complicated expressions of the parties, and later help them express their often vaguely expressed goals in clear and simple terms.

A mediator's facility with language also becomes crucial as the parties near agreement. "Have you ever asked a participant why they're willing to enter into a certain agreement and have them say 'I don't know'"? asks Jim Melamed. "Of course not, because people will not agree to do something until they can explain to themselves why it is good for them to do it. Putting into words the rationale that will support them in making this agreement is the job of the mediator. It's the sermonette thing; it gives the participants cover, a face-saving rationale that supports them in being more flexible than they anticipated being."

"Unrestrained," notes Melamed, "these same language skills can be dangerous because they can be used to talk participants into doing things that are really not in their best interest. This is, of course, why mediators have strict ethical requirements for impartiality and neutrality."

Mediators also need good language skills to draft the agreement. In larger cases, you may just outline the terms and instruct the parties to take it to their lawyers, accountants, or other advisers for review. But in smaller cases, you'll actually draft the agreement, and careful use of language is essential. I usually do a first draft in longhand with both sides sitting in front of me, reading aloud each provision as I write. I try to express exactly what the parties have agreed to, without any mention of fault or blame. The writing needs to be concise enough so the document stays reasonably short and understandable, but it has to contain enough detail so its meaning is clear to the parties not only today—after they've just spent three hours discussing the issues in detail—but three years from now, when they refer to it long after their memories of the discussion have faded.

A facility with language is essential for the mediator, from the beginning of the process all the way to the end. Some innate language ability and comfort with language is necessary, although if basic skills are present, they can be further developed through good mediator training.

A Calm Demeanor

Parties in mediation are under stress. They are, after all, sitting across the table from the person or persons whom they see as the source of their problem. The mediator, therefore, needs to be able to project a sense of calm to help them feel safe and relaxed enough to participate in the mediation. As Melamed puts it,

Some people have their idle set very high. There is a certain frenetic pace to how they conduct themselves, and I'd say those people are not going to end up as the best mediators. Mediation requires you to create a certain contemplative environment, with the discussion often moving at the rate of the slowest participant.

Having said that, the mediator cannot be too laid-back without draining all the energy out of the session. A calm but purposeful demeanor seems to work best.

Related to a calm personality is, as mediator Michael Lang pointed out earlier, an ability to deal with ambiguity. A good mediator must be comfortable discussing, sometimes for hours, a situation in which it may never be found who did what to whom or who was right and who was wrong (indeed, issues of fault are mostly irrelevant to the process). And negotiations will proceed in great detail, even as several very different avenues toward possible settlement remain open and under discussion simultaneously. One has to be comfortable dealing with this kind of uncertainty. If you get ruffled by it or are easily put on edge, your discomfort may affect the parties and undercut the chances for a successful outcome.

Ability to Understand Complex Facts

A mediator needs to be able to understand the sometimes complicated fact patterns involved in a case, so a reasonable degree of abstract reasoning and intelligence is necessary. I purposely didn't use the expression *fast on your feet*, however, because although you have to be fast enough to think of the next strategic question, you don't have to be so quick to think of all the answers. Mediation is not a debating society where you're trying to outsmart the other people in the room; you can slow down the session to give yourself time to consider what you've heard and process the information. You can do this by letting the parties talk about tangential subjects while you digest what you've heard; you can take a break before and after going into caucus; or you can simply say you need to call a recess to consider what you've heard and then schedule another session for the following week.

Trustworthiness in Keeping Confidences

Keeping confidences is the currency of a good mediator; without the ability to keep confidences, no one can, or should, be mediating. Keeping confidences may sound easy if you haven't been put to the test. But mediators face this challenge both inside and outside the hearing room. Inside the session, the mediator is meeting in private caucus with each party and receiving sensitive information that must not be revealed to the other side unless the party who told it gives specific permission. After one or two rounds of caucuses, knocking around in the mediator's head is a fairly complex list of things revealed by both sides, some of which the mediator may have permission to reveal but much of which must be kept secret. Keeping all that straight while in the midst of conducting negotiations toward a settlement is no easy task.

But even tougher sometimes is protecting the confidence of your clients outside the session—protecting it absolutely. That means not even revealing who the participants in a case might have been. I have had the privilege—and challenge—of mediating sensitive personal matters with people well known to others in my family and being prohibited from revealing to anyone, even my wife, that I had even met with these people. In this regard, the mediator carries the same burdens of confidentiality that a therapist, lawyer, or clergy person does. And in the unlikely event you are called to testify in a court of law or arbitration proceeding and asked to reveal information about what was said in the mediation session, your clients and the entire profession of mediation will be relying on you to refuse to breach that oath of confidentiality, regardless of what the personal cost to you might be. Think carefully about whether this is a professional burden you are willing to undertake.

Professional Detachment

As a mediator, you will be privy to an intimate look into the lives of your clients. You will see their pain, their dashed hopes, their life-transforming injuries, their wrecked marriages, and ruined businesses. You can assist them by moving them through a process that has been proven helpful. But ultimately, you can't change their lives. And once the mediation is over, you are powerless to do more. They are unlikely to ever talk with you about the matter again.

Some people are good at maintaining a professional detachment from their clients' lives so that once a session is over, they close the file and move on to the next case. Other people are unable to do this; they get too wrapped up in the lives of their clients and just cannot let go. They feel an overwhelming temptation to follow up, to try to be of further help, even just to find out what happened next.

Moreover, no mediator succeeds all the time. One of the frustrations of being a mediator is that one has no control over the facts in dispute or the attitudes of the disputants. Some cases, due to especially thorny issues or especially thorny people, just cannot be successfully mediated, even with the finest mediator doing a first-rate job. In such cases, the good mediator will close the hearing without a settlement and be able to accept the result without seeing it as a personal failing.

If you are, by nature, so sensitive that you cannot let go and detach from clients' lives or accept an unsatisfactory outcome to a case, mediation may not be for you. It could be too painful, and ultimately you might get yourself into trouble for violating professional ethics.

Sense of Humor and Sense of Drama

Mediators often use humor to relieve tension during a session. Telling a joke or a humorous story is a good way to distract the parties when they get off track or when anxiety is so high they cannot continue with a rational discussion. But humor can also backfire or be offensive if it's not done well, so having a sense for the appropriateness and timing of humor is important.

A related skill is what I would call a sense of the drama in mediation. As I noted earlier, a mediation session has a setting: the conference room, the table and chairs, the blank pads of paper. And there's a cast of characters: you, the disputants, their supporters or friends. And then there's a plot: the six-stage process leading, ideally, to a resolution. The opening lines of the drama—the mediator's opening statement—are yours, but thereafter you must lead the parties through this dramatic encounter. The skill with which you do this depends in part on your sense of the drama inherent in the process. As the "director," you must decide, for example, how much to allow the tension to build before diffusing it with a distracting joke or story, how hard to push during caucus to move a party off an initial demand, how to present a new idea for settlement, and, in the later stages, when to cue the parties that a shift in negotiating position would be helpful.

A sense of humor is inborn, and although some of the sense of the drama of mediation can be learned in training, I think much of it, like the ability to read participants, is innate.

Patience and Perseverance

Even more than in many other professions, mediation requires patience and perseverance. This is because no matter how good you are at the job and how hard you work, there are always at least two other people in the room whose attitudes, actions, and words you cannot control. You may come to see after just an hour of mediation a clear path toward resolution of the parties' dispute, but it may take them many more hours or days or weeks to get there. In the meantime, you have to persevere in your efforts, patiently and calmly.

I find my own patience most often taxed during the middle and later stages of a session when the parties may insist on raising lots of minor issues, all of which have to be laboriously worked through before you can get them to focus on the major one and resolve it. Often there comes a time when whatever goodwill the parties came in with seems to have disappeared, and one or even both of them threaten to leave. Another testing point often comes toward the end of the session when the parties have reached a settlement in principle but insist on repeated changes in the wording of the agreement. It's been reported, for example, that to satisfy Israeli and Egyptian negotiators, President Carter and his mediation team at Camp David drafted no fewer than twenty-three versions of a proposed peace agreement.[4] In his diary, Carter wrote, "I resolve to do everything possible to get out of the negotiating business."[5] Fortunately, President Carter persevered in his work as a mediator, and since he left office has helped settle many international disputes. Still, the frustration he expressed is something with which many mediators can identify and something those thinking of entering the field should consider.

Self-Marketing and Political Skills

I know many people who paid for and successfully completed mediator training, rented an office, bought furniture and equipment, took a listing in the Yellow Pages, and then sat back waiting for the phone to ring. After a year, they still had not mediated a single case. They are among the naive victims of a common delusion: that lots of people are just waiting to come to a mediator to settle their disputes.

It's true, of course, that loads of disputes could be settled by a mediator. The problem is that most people never think of picking up the phone and calling one. Mediation is still too new. So until such time as mediators are as popular as lawyers, successful mediators will need an entrepreneurial spirit. If you want the phone to ring, you're going to have to get out there and market your services to the people who can be your clients or who can refer clients to you.

Some people have the personality for doing this; they like meeting people and are natural self-promoters. Others shy away from these activities; for them, the process is painful and often unsuccessful. Yet the reality of the marketplace, especially private practice, requires a lot of self-promotion.

For example, if you are thinking of a private practice in family and divorce mediation, you'll need to send letters of introduction to people who can refer cases to you—therapists, clergy, and lawyers. Then you'll need to follow up with phone calls, meetings, and lunches, and arrange opportunities to speak about mediation to groups at community centers, churches, and social clubs. If your interest lies more in business mediation, you'll need to go through the same process with people such as business owners, accountants, consultants, lawyers, and officials from the chamber of commerce.

Private practice also requires good political skills, such as the ability to make and maintain long-term business contacts, to scope out the competition, and to maintain comfortable relations with other mediators in your community, even as you remain competitors.

Political skills are also essential if you're planning to work within an institution—a court system, school, or large business. To understand how the institution works and how to navigate layers of management, you'll need good political instincts. Your survival and professional growth within the organization will depend on it. We'll talk more about these aspects of mediation practice in Chapters Six and Seven, but it's worth keeping in mind that if you don't have the ability or desire to sell yourself, private practice is probably not for you. In any type of practice, good political skills are essential.

AT A GLANCE

Desired Skills and Personality Traits

- Good Listening Skills

- Ability to "Read" People

- Facility with Language

- A Calm Demeanor

- Ability to Understand Complex Facts

- Trustworthiness in Keeping Confidences

- Professional Detachment

- Sense of Humor and Sense of Drama

- Patience and Perseverance

- Self-Marketing and Political Skills

CONCLUSION

I've attempted to identify some of the personality traits and skills common to successful mediators. Some of these you can learn in a good training program. Others tend to be innate; some people have them and others do not. Yet as I emphasized earlier, some mediators lack many of these traits but have other abilities—call them intuitive peace-making skills—that nevertheless allow them to succeed as mediators.

I remember one man with whom I took basic mediator training, for instance. He was not particularly good with language; I'm not sure if he even graduated from high school. And it was difficult for him to understand the details of complex factual disputes. Further, some of the techniques of good listening that we had practiced in class seemed to elude him; for example, he wasn't good at rephrasing the parties' statements to confirm he'd heard what they had said. And I don't recall him having much of a sense of humor. Nevertheless, I watched repeatedly as this man succeeded in helping settle cases. Looking back, I think what allowed him to succeed was his kindness. He had an essential humanity about him—an innate goodness, if you will—and the longer you sat at the table with him the more you felt it and wanted to honor it by being good and kind yourself. I think in his presence people felt compelled to compromise in order to end their conflict.

So use the list as best you can to evaluate yourself as a potential mediator, but bear in mind that no list is definitive. The only way to know for sure if you would be a good mediator and enjoy the work is to get some basic training and try your hand at a few cases. In the next chapter, we'll look at different kinds of training programs and how you can select training that is best suited to your needs.

5

Mediator Training

To those who have never done it, mediation can look deceptively easy: you just sit at the head of the table and talk sense to people until they agree to be reasonable. It can look so easy, in fact, that some people make the mistake of thinking they can mediate without being trained. This is nearly always a mistake. Over the years, I've seen prominent people—judges, community leaders, respected clergy—attempt to mediate high-profile, public disputes, only to get tripped up and land themselves and the disputants into an even worse mess.

If you want to mediate, you need to be trained. It's that simple. But fortunately, mediator training is usually a stimulating, enjoyable experience. Many people, in fact, who never intend to mediate take the training anyway just to learn the skills, which they can always use in their regular jobs or personal lives.

As mediation has grown in popularity, mediator training has become a good-size industry. My own quick review of advertisements for training in mediation journals and similar media shows nearly a 50 percent increase in course listings over the past five years. Training is offered through community mediation centers, private dispute resolution companies, and colleges and universities; a growing number of independent trainers travel around the country giving seminars. Training quality varies with the trainers, the sponsoring organization, and the group of people being trained.

Which training you take, where you take it, and with whom are important considerations. In this chapter, we'll examine basic mediator training, divorce mediation and other specialized training, and degree programs in dispute resolution. We'll also examine the issues of licensing and the certifying of mediators.

BASIC MEDIATOR TRAINING

A word of caution: many people get enthusiastic about mediation and want to jump right into a specialty area—often divorce mediation because it's well known—and open a private practice. Try to avoid yielding to the impulse. Too often, enthusiasts take an expensive, specialized training course—sometimes traveling hundreds of miles to do so—only to find later that they wasted their time and money. After handling just a few cases, they discover they aren't particularly good at mediating or, even if are, they just don't enjoy it.

To avoid this situation, I urge you not to begin your mediation career with specialized or expensive training but instead to begin with a program of low-cost, basic training. By *basic training*, I mean an introductory course that covers—through lectures, demonstrations, videos, and role plays—the essentials of mediation: the psychology of human conflict, negotiation theory, techniques of listening and speaking, laws of mediation and confidentiality, mediator ethics, and the practical skills needed to conduct a mediation session.

To acquire these skills, I recommend you take advantage of one of the best training deals available: a twenty-five to forty-hour basic mediator training course at a nonprofit community mediation center. As we discussed in Chapter Three, community mediation centers are tax-supported agencies that provide free or low-cost mediation services to the general public. There are hundreds of centers nationwide; check the Yellow Pages under "mediation" and you'll probably find one where you live or close by. Fifteen years ago, I took my first mediator training at a public mediation center, the Center for Dispute Settlement in Rochester, New York, and I remain confident today that it was the best way to get started.

To be sure, private, for-profit training companies will also teach you the basics of mediation. Their fees, however, will be substantial— probably $1,000 or more. A community mediation center will charge half that amount or less. Some centers even train people for free in exchange for promising to volunteer their time as mediators for a set number of hours during the following year. (Some centers charge a fee for their training but then rebate it after you fulfill the volunteer commitment.)

Beyond cost savings, the best reason to get trained at a community mediation center is that only the centers offer a post-training apprenticeship where you can practice your new skills on real cases. Private firms may offer good-quality training, but they can't offer you real cases to mediate.

"Once you get out of that training, you're not ready to mediate," advises Craig Coletta, coordinator for the National Association for Community Mediation, a group that represents nearly three hundred centers in forty-seven states. "You've learned the skills, but you have no fluency in them. Apprenticeship gives trainees the opportunity to apply mediation skills in real situations in a way they can't learn just in role plays" (personal communication, April 2000).

As noted in Chapter Three, community mediation centers these days handle a mix of neighborhood, consumer, small-business, minor criminal, and family disputes, so during your apprenticeship—and later as a volunteer—you're likely to face a range of challenging cases on which to practice the skills you learned in the classroom. We'll talk more about what happens during the apprenticeship after we take a look at what you can expect in typical, basic training at a community mediation center.

> **TRAINING RULE 1: START WITH A BASIC MEDIATOR TRAINING AT A COMMUNITY MEDIATION CENTER TO FIND OUT IF YOU LIKE MEDIATING AND ARE ANY GOOD AT IT.**

WHAT TO EXPECT IN BASIC TRAINING

As noted, basic mediator training generally consists of twenty-five to forty hours of class time. The number of hours will depend on local rules and whether state law sets a minimum. (In California, Florida, Michigan, New York, and Texas, for example, state laws or court rules set minimum training requirements for those who mediate in state-funded centers.) Years ago, twenty-five hours was typical, but today, as more topics like cross-cultural differences and mediator ethics are added to the curriculum, forty hours is emerging as the standard. Training is usually held on five consecutive weekdays or sometimes over two or three weekends.

Community mediation centers need a steady supply of volunteers to handle their caseload and have found that the best way to maintain a pool of volunteers is to constantly train new candidates. Consequently, if you call a center today, you can probably be scheduled for training within the next couple of months. Note, however, that some centers accept more people for training than they can accommodate in their apprenticeship program. I know one center where trainees currently wait a full year for a case. Before signing up for training, confirm with the center that they have an apprenticeship program and will guarantee you cases on which to practice.

At community mediation centers, training is usually conducted by staff members, often assisted by some of the center's own experienced mediators. I have seen excellent training; some is just adequate. It's fair to say that at some centers, particularly the smaller ones, the quality of individual trainers may not be as consistently high as you would find with full-time, professional trainers at for-profit firms. Still, the other advantages of training at a community mediation center— low cost, accessibility, and opportunity for apprenticeship—in my opinion outweigh concerns about the quality of individual trainers. In fact, the use of multiple trainers at most centers offers its own advantage: you get to hear about mediation from a variety of points of view. Anyway, if you complete the training and apprenticeship and find you like mediation, you can always take a more advanced training with some of the outstanding national or regional trainers.

One nice aspect of training at a community mediation center is the diverse mix of people you're likely to find there. At one session I attended recently, there were thirteen trainees, ranging in age from about twenty to seventy. Among them were two college students, a retired social worker, a mechanical engineer, the director of a service program for mentally disabled adults, the human resources director of a large business corporation, a financial planner, a librarian, a paralegal, a community activist, and an accountant. Only a few of those attending aimed to become professional mediators; most just wanted to volunteer as mediators or hoped to acquire new skills to enhance their present jobs. For example, the financial planner wanted mediation skills to use in helping clients' families deal with conflicts over financial goals; the paralegal believed she could mediate minor harassment cases that come through the law office where she works; the community activist hoped negotiating skills would help her deal more effectively with local government officials. One trainee had just completed basic mediator training with a private firm but realized he had no opportunity to test out his skills. He was taking basic training all over again at the community mediation center in order to participate in the apprenticeship program.

Content of the Training

Your training course is likely to begin with a set of exercises designed to get you thinking about conflict. In the session I attended recently, trainees were asked to think of metaphors for conflict. They suggested a boxing match (requiring a mediator as referee to be sure the punches land fairly), a raging fire (requiring a mediator as firefighter to extinguish it), and an upset stomach (mediation is like Pepto Bismol). Eventually, the group recognized that conflict is not always bad and can often lead to growth and change.

From another training session, I recall an exercise called "family dining table," which was meant to reveal how our upbringing may influence our attitudes toward conflict. Trainees are given paper and crayons and asked to draw the table where their family usually ate dinner, draw each person at the table, and then draw lines between each person showing how the conversation went—smooth lines for relaxed talk, jagged lines for tense talk or arguments. When I did this exercise, I found myself drawing lines of tension back and forth between my father and my older brother and between my mother and my older sister, but few lines connecting any of them to me. Looking at what I'd drawn, I realized that as the youngest in the family, I'd sat night after night at the dinner table, for the most part quietly observing the conflict around me—not unlike what I do as a mediator.

Another common opening exercise asks trainees to view a simple line drawing that depicts, depending on how you look at it, either a young girl or an old woman. In the training I recently observed, half the group saw the young girl and several saw the old woman, but a few others saw what they insisted was a rabbit; one person claimed to see a convertible with its hood up, driving off a cliff. The trainer effectively used the exercise to illustrate how reasonable people can look at the same thing but see it differently, just as the parties in mediation will insist on their own versions of the truth in their dispute. "Perception is a person's reality," stressed the trainer. "It is their truth." The group then generated a list of factors that can affect people's perceptions: age, gender, ethnicity, religion, culture, education, and socioeconomic status.

A related exercise I've seen is designed to reveal one's own prejudices. The trainer describes a fictitious person: her looks, clothes, occupation, and manner of speech. Trainees are then asked to answer a series of questions about the personal habits, family life, political beliefs, and financial situation of the person described. When trainees compare their answers, they find that what they have described are simply their own assumptions and prejudices about people. The exercise helps teach mediators to be aware of their own prejudices, particularly during the opening stages of mediation when one may be tempted to form opinions of the disputants based on appearance or superficial information.

In communities with ethnically diverse populations, significant training time may be spent on how cultural differences can affect conflict and communication. In some Asian cultures, for example, making direct eye contact is considered disrespectful, but in mainstream American culture, avoiding direct eye contact is considered suspect. Put people from both cultures at the same mediation table, and one may think the other is being disrespectful while the other thinks the first is lying. Similarly, mainstream American culture assumes that a mediator, in order to be neutral and credible, should be unknown to both parties. But people from some other cultures would consider that ridiculous. How can you help solve our problem, they might ask, if you don't know either of us?

Another focus of exercises early in training will be communication skills, specifically, listening and speaking. To sharpen listening skills—and get to know each other—trainees, working in pairs, might be asked to tell each other their life stories in two minutes of nonstop talking. The listeners will then be asked to repeat back as much of the story as they can recall.

In another exercise about how we send and receive messages, a trainer I recently observed walked calmly over to one young man who was seated among the trainees, then suddenly leaned into his face and screamed, *"Jim, I'm not angry at you!"* Studies have found, the trainer explained, that communication is 55 percent tone of voice, 38 percent body language, and just 7 percent words.

Basic training will include a comparison of the various methods of dispute resolution, including negotiation, fact finding, conciliation, mediation, arbitration, and litigation. Some of the legal issues in mediation will be discussed: rules of confidentiality and how they apply to mediators, what a mediator should do if information received during the hearing suggests child or spouse abuse (the answer depends on state law), and how to help parties write a settlement agreement that will be legally binding.

It's interesting, by the way, to notice what's not included in the training: the basics of family law, consumer law, or property rights. Even though these issues are likely to arise in cases typically heard at community mediation centers, it's not the mediator's role to act as lawyer or judge, and mediator training isn't law school. When these matters do come up in an actual case, mediators mostly have to rely on their own general knowledge or be able to pick up the basics from the parties themselves or in consultation with the center's staff. (Training for divorce mediation does include instruction in family law, tax law, and other relevant areas. Divorce mediator training is discussed in a later section.)

In a typical twenty-five or forty-hour basic training course, fully half the time will likely be spent learning and practicing the skills to conduct a two-party mediation. (Multiparty mediation is usually reserved for more advanced training.) Lectures will be supported by videos of actual or simulated cases and role plays in which you will get to try out your skills on mock cases. In role plays, trainees will break up into groups of three or four, each taking the part of one of the participants in a simulated mediation:

- The mediator

- The claimant (the person who first brings the dispute to a mediation center)

- The respondent (the person with whom the claimant has a dispute)

- A witness (brought to the mediation by either side)

Some of the role plays will be designed to improve listening and negotiating skills, to reveal personal prejudices, or to develop an ability to detect hidden interpersonal conflicts among the parties.

In a typical role play, for example, the trainee playing the mediator is told that the case involves a property-line dispute between two neighbors—a man and a woman. What the trainee is not told, however, is that the two neighbors many years ago were close friends but then had a falling out when the wife of one quarreled with the husband of the other over child-rearing issues. The dispute about the property line, although real, is just the latest expression of continuing distrust between the neighbors because of the earlier break in their friendship. In the mock mediation, the trainees playing the feuding neighbors know this, but the trainee playing the mediator does not and must discover it through careful listening and questioning. The goal is not to make the neighbors friends again but to help them come to terms with the break in their relationship so they can not only resolve this property-line dispute but can agree to live as neighbors without further disputes erupting. This type of role play helps sharpen important skills a mediator will need to resolve real cases.

Basic training may conclude with a session on how to help the parties draft an effective settlement agreement, a discussion of mediator ethics, and the record-keeping requirements of the particular mediation center where the trainees will apprentice as volunteer mediators.

Apprenticeship

Apprenticeship usually begins with the trainees observing experienced mediators as they hear actual cases. Typically, centers require silent observation of three or more mediations. The trainee attends with the permission of the disputants and is bound by the same rules of confidentiality as the mediator. This experience exposes the trainee to different styles of mediation and to some of the issues that come up in real cases.

The next step is co-mediation. During an actual mediation, the trainee sits next to the experienced mediator and practices conducting various parts of the session. The trainee may, for example, deliver the opening statement—the first stage of mediation in which the purpose of and rules for mediation are explained to the parties.

The final step of the apprenticeship comes when trainees are allowed to "solo," that is, to mediate cases on their own. An experienced mediator observes the session and steps in if the trainee needs help. The observer takes notes on the trainee's technique to review with him or her afterwards. Several solo mediations may be scheduled until both the trainee and the staff of the mediation center feel confident that the trainee can handle cases alone.

When the apprenticeship is completed, the trainee is ready to mediate. (If watching a few cases and then handling a few under supervision doesn't sound like a lot of preparation, consider that lawyers can go into court alone on their first day after being admitted to the bar without ever having set foot in a courtroom or handling a case under the supervision of an experienced attorney.)

DIVORCE MEDIATION AND OTHER SPECIALIZED TRAINING

As noted in Chapter One, most people who make a full- or part-time career in mediation today do so as divorce mediators. The demand for divorce mediation has been strong and continues to grow.

In theory, anyone can hang out a shingle and declare him- or herself to be a divorce mediator, but if it's a mistake—as I believe it is—to attempt to do general mediation without training, it's an even bigger mistake to try to be a divorce mediator without training. Mediating divorces requires an understanding of family law, tax law, pensions, domestic violence, child development, and the psychology of families in crisis—to name just a few complex subjects. Divorce mediators deal with couples at one of the worst and most emotionally charged times of their lives. Divorce mediation is nothing to play around with. An untrained mediator can cause great harm, not only to the divorcing couple but to their children as well.

If you aim to become a divorce mediator, you absolutely must acquire the necessary knowledge and skills to do it well, and the best way to do that—and the only way I recommend—is by taking a training course approved by the Association for Conflict Resolution (ACR).

The ACR is a national, nonprofit organization that sets standards for the training and practice of divorce and family mediation. (ACR is a merged organization of the former Academy of Family Mediators, CREnet, and the Society of Professionals in Dispute Resolution.) Training programs approved by ACR must meet detailed, minimum requirements for course content and presentation.

An ACR-approved training course for divorce mediation must do the following:

- Include forty hours of instruction spread over a minimum of five days

- Include at least six hours of role play

- Provide trainees with a comprehensive manual of written materials and forms

- Teach general mediation skills with demonstrations and role plays focused on family issues

- Instruct how to screen for domestic violence

- Address the consequences of separation and divorce on adults and children, and cover issues of parenting, division of marital assets and liabilities, spousal maintenance and child support, insurance, pensions, and tax filing.

Expect to pay between $1,000 and $1,500 for ACR-approved training. Some trainers offer a slight discount if you sign up early and pay the full fee in advance.

In addition to forty-hour divorce mediation training, the ACR also approves thirty-hour training courses in family mediation that cover parenting, custody, and other family matters, but omit the financial issues covered in divorce mediation training. Fees for family mediation training are likely to be 20 to 30 percent lower than those for divorce mediation training.

Some years ago, I took a full forty-hour, ACR-approved training course with the intention of doing divorce mediation. But even before the training was completed, I knew I would not mediate divorces. I just found it too painful to deal with some of the issues, particularly those involving children. I have high regard for mediators who help divorcing couples through such a difficult time, but I could not do it. I also saw that being a competent divorce mediator would require me to keep up with pension and tax laws, and local court decisions involving spousal maintenance, child support, and custody. With my other obligations, I knew I could not devote the necessary time and attention to those topics.

If you're unsure about pursuing this aspect of mediation, the ACR has some excellent materials to show you in more detail what divorce mediation looks like. On request, they will send a brochure, "Mediation," that contains general information. The ACR also has a twenty-minute videotape, "Mediation: It's Up to You." The tape simulates a mediation between a couple who have one small child and also own a business together. (The session is simulated, but the mediator is a real, nationally recognized divorce mediator.) The tape is available for $59.95—a bargain if it helps you make a clear decision about whether or not to take training that lasts five days and costs upwards of $1,000.

Perhaps not surprisingly, many people get interested in becoming divorce mediators after having had their own divorces mediated. It's as good an introduction to the field as any, I suppose. Some mediation trainers caution, however, that you should wait a while before going ahead with training. They want you to be sure your attraction to the field is a genuine career move and not just an emotional reaction to your own divorce.

SELECTING A TRAINING COURSE

When the ACR approves a training course, technically it approves only the course content; it does not endorse the individual trainer. Nevertheless, even to submit a course for ACR approval, a trainer must meet the criteria for practitioner-level status in the ACR. This means the trainer has taken at least sixty hours of ACR-approved training, had a minimum of one hundred hours of face-to-face mediation experience, had sample case reports reviewed by other mediators, and completed twenty hours of continuous education every two years.

At present, the ACR maintains a list of about fifty trainers around the country who offer approved courses. The list shows trainers based in about twenty states and several Canadian provinces. Some offer training on a regular schedule outside their home states, and some will conduct a training anywhere if a person interested in being trained can recruit a minimum number of participants (usually four to six). To obtain the ACR's current list of trainers offering approved courses, contact the ACR: The Association for Conflict Resolution, 1527 New Hampshire Ave., NW, Washington, DC 20036; (202) 667–9700, fax: (202) 265–1968, Web address: www.acresolution.org.

> **TRAINING RULE 2: IF YOU WANT TO BECOME A DIVORCE MEDIATOR, TAKE TRAINING APPROVED BY THE ASSOCIATION FOR CONFLICT RESOLUTION.**

Once you obtain the ACR's list of trainers, take some time to consider which trainer to use. Obviously, location and cost will be factors, but selecting someone to train you in divorce mediation should involve more than just considerations of cost and location.

Your trainer will in many ways shape your early practice and may become an important long-term mentor, supervising your early case work so you can later qualify for ACR membership.

GUIDELINES FOR CHOOSING A DIVORCE MEDIATION TRAINER

If possible, try to meet the prospective trainer—or at least talk on the phone—before signing up. Does the personal chemistry feel right? Does the trainer seem enthusiastic or somewhat stale after mediating and training for decades?

Get a sense for the trainer's focus. Does the trainer emphasize the economics of divorce or the parenting and emotional aspects? How does the trainer's approach compare with what you anticipate will be your own? You and the trainer don't have to have the same approach—complementary interests can be good—but it's useful to know going in whether you differ or not.

Ask for references to others who have completed training with this trainer and who are now practicing.

If the trainer lives in your town, ask how the trainer works with trainees who set up practice locally. Soon you will be direct competitors for the same clientele. Is the trainer supportive of this?

Will the trainer's manual include forms for you to use in setting up and marketing your own practice? (You can purchase these elsewhere, but it's cheaper if the trainer provides them in the manual.)

Whether it's better to get trained inside your home community or outside is an interesting question. On the one hand, a trainer from outside your community may give you a broader view of the field and fresher marketing ideas than someone who lives in the same town. On the other hand, a local trainer will be familiar with local court rules and client referral sources such as therapists, clergy, and divorce lawyers. If the trainer is willing to share these with you to help you get started, that can be valuable.

Yet I wonder about the large number of people who take divorce mediation training but never practice. The ACR estimates that about fifty thousand people have taken ACR-approved training over the years, but only about half are currently practicing. I understand some, like myself, choosing not to practice because they find they're uneasy with the emotional aspects of divorce, and others finding they just don't care for the work or aren't successful at it. I wonder, however, if some trainers, concerned about too much local competition, subtly influence their own trainees not to go into practice, perhaps by making aspects of the work seem too daunting. I don't know the answer, but in selecting a trainer, I'd give that possibility some thought.

OTHER SPECIALIZED TRAINING

In addition to divorce and family mediation, there are opportunities for specialized training in areas in which you may have a particular interest. Remember, training for this type of work should come only after you complete a basic mediator training and get some experience as an apprentice and volunteer.

Next are listed some of the more popular areas, just to give a sense of what is available. Most specialty training is offered by either private training firms, conflict resolution groups, or professional associations.

Health Care

The growing number of disputes arising out of the delivery of health care services has created a demand for conflict resolution in this field. Cases involve claims against physicians, hospitals, and health maintenance organizations, disputes between physicians and insurers, and grievances among health care workers and their employers.

Several programs are available to train people to mediate health care disputes. One, offered by the American Health Lawyers Association, is open to both lawyers and nonlawyers.

Physicians, nurses, and health care executives are among those who have participated. For information, contact the American Health Lawyers Association at (202) 833–1100 or visit their Web site: www.healthlawyers.org.

Courses to help health professionals improve negotiation and conflict resolution skills are offered by the Harvard School of Public Health. Recent classes have included simulated exercises modeling bioethical conflicts, interhospital disputes, interprofessional disputes and community health matters. For information on current course offerings, contact the school at (617) 496–0865 or through their Web site: www.hsph.harvard.edu.

Environment and Public Policy

Issues such as land use, zoning, environmental protection, and the siting of highways and public buildings come under the general heading of "public policy" disputes. Many colleges that offer advanced degrees in conflict resolution also offer courses on mediating environmental and public policy disputes. One private training firm, CDR Associates of Boulder, Colorado, offers several courses regularly on these topics. Contact CDR at 1–800-Mediate or through their Web site: www.mediate.org.

Employment

Workplace disputes involving termination, discrimination, and other labor-management issues are an increasing part of the mediation caseload nationally. The U.S. Equal Employment Opportunity Commission trains mediators to hear cases brought before the agency. Contact the EEOC at the agency's national headquarters in Washington, D.C. at (202) 663–4900 or through their Web site: www.eeoc.gov. Private training firms such as CDR Associates also offer training programs on mediating workplace disputes. Special training to mediate cases involving individuals with disabilities is available through the Institute for ADA Mediation at the University of Louisville College of Business and Public Administration in Louisville, Kentucky. Contact the institute at (502) 458–9675.

Real Estate

The National Association of Realtors trains association members to mediate disputes such as those concerning fee splitting between realtors. Contact the association at (800) 874–6500 or at their Web site: www.nar.realtor.com.

Securities

The National Association of Securities Dealers (NASD) trains mediators to resolve disputes between brokers and between brokers and customers. Lawyers, managers of stock brokerages, and people who have been professional arbitrators are among the three hundred people who have been trained. The three-day training programs cost about $700 and are held in major cities around the country. For information, contact the NASD's mediation program office at (212) 858–3915 or through their Web site: www.nasdadr.com.

On-Line Mediation

A relatively new area of specialty involves the procedures and techniques used in on-line mediation. Training programs cover Internet technology, use of text, images, audio, threaded discussions, use of on-line conference rooms, and issues of confidentiality. For current training opportunities, contact individual on-line dispute resolution firms (see Chapter Six) or go to the Web site: www.mediate.com.

Some of the groups mentioned may require you to have completed a basic mediator training course before enrolling in their specialized training; others will accept you without prior training. Regardless, I still recommend you get basic training and some experience at a community mediation center before moving into a specialty area.

DEGREE PROGRAMS IN
DISPUTE RESOLUTION

An increasing number of colleges and universities now grant master's degrees and even doctorates in conflict resolution. These programs can require years of work and cost tens of thousands of dollars. Are they worth it? Before we consider that question, let's see what some of these programs offer.

Schools with Degree Programs

I'm not aware of any schools that grant undergraduate degrees in conflict resolution, although an increasing number do offer what are called certificate programs, roughly equivalent to a "minor." For example, a school may offer a bachelor's or master's degree in psychology, education, or business with a certificate in dispute resolution.

But the list of schools offering graduate programs in conflict resolution is growing rapidly. Three of the better-known programs are at George Mason University, Antioch University McGregor, and Nova University. We'll take a closer look at each.

George Mason University. One of the first schools to offer a master's degree in conflict resolution was George Mason University, located in Fairfax, Virginia, just outside Washington, D.C. Since 1982 when the program began, more than two hundred students have received Master of Science degrees in conflict analysis and resolution. Since 1988, a related doctoral program has produced nearly twenty Ph.D's.

The M.S. degree is intended as a two-year program requiring forty-one credit hours. Total tuition and fees are about $22,000 for out-of-state and international students and about half that for in-state residents. Room and board are extra.

Mediation and conflict resolution tends to be a midcareer field, explains Frank Blechman, coordinator of the M.S. degree program at George Mason. "The program favors mature learners. The ideal candidate is someone who brings us a lot of experience." Blechman says the average age for entering master's students is thirty-two, "but that means some students are twenty-two and others are forty-two. We even had one doctoral student who entered at age seventy-two" (personal communication, April 2000).

The George Mason program seeks to integrate conflict resolution theory and practices such as negotiation, mediation, and third-party consultation. Given the school's proximity to the nation's capital, students enjoy a rich variety of internships and field practice opportunities. "Students work as part of a team with the faculty, intervening in local and regional conflicts," explains Blechman. "Graduate students recently have participated in dialogues between police and youth gangs and worked with ombudsmen at the National Institutes of Health and other government agencies. We are also beginning to offer more international field opportunities."

Where do graduates of the program work after receiving their master's degrees? According to Blechman,

> about a third put their new skills to work in their existing jobs as mid-level managers in government and private business; another third run programs for organizations dealing with conflict situations, both domestically and around the world; about 15 percent wind up doing something that looks like mediation practice—either mediating or running a mediation service—and the rest become involved in miscellaneous pursuits.

Of the doctoral graduates, adds Blechman, most but not all go on to teach. Of the others, one works in Atlanta with the Carter Center, an organization established by former President Jimmy Carter to promote conflict resolution. One works with an international human rights program in London; and one, a Native American, is working to reestablish traditional dispute resolution structures among tribes.

Antioch University McGregor

Another school that was early to offer a degree program in conflict resolution is Antioch University McGregor in Ohio. Students who complete the school's Master of Arts degree in conflict resolution have received "a solid theoretical grounding in the literature of the discipline and a strong skill base of the very best practices in the field," writes Kathy Hale (personal communication, June 2000), professor and chair of the graduate program in conflict resolution.

Antioch's current program involves a mix of courses and clinical experiences, including

- Introduction to Conflict Studies and Intervention
- Identity, Culture, and Conflict
- Negotiation
- Mediation
- Research Methods
- Introduction to Theories of Conflict and Resolution
- Communication and Conflict
- Group Decision Making and Conflict Processes
- Advanced Theory and Practice of Third-Party Intervention
- Marketing Workshop
- Training Workshop

"I was one of the younger people in the program," recalls Beth Danehy, who was in her early thirties when she started the Antioch program in 1996. "Most were midcareer people. They came from all over the country and internationally" (personal communication, June 2000).

Danehy, who lives in upstate New York, took advantage of Antioch's "limited residency" program under which (at that time) she needed to be on the Antioch campus only three weeks out of a year. Beyond that, she could communicate long-distance with her professors and create internships and independent studies to fulfill the course requirements.

Later the Antioch program was redesigned. Currently, students are on-campus two weeks in their first year and two weeks in their second year. At other times, they take a series of on-line courses offered by Antioch faculty, do clinical work in their own communities, and have the option of an intensive, ten-hour course in lieu of a thesis. Most students complete the program in two years.

Danehy received her master's degree in 2000. As to why it took her five years to complete what for many is a two-year program, Danehy explains, "Life happened. I got married and had twins." She says she paid "about $40,000" in tuition, fees, and living costs, although students completing the degree in two years would pay closer to $25,000.

"I'd recommend the program to people who want to have more education for their own growth as mediators," says Danehy, who now is director of communications and professional relations for a local office of the Realtors Association. She also oversees the group's conflict resolution program. "From my experience, the degree gives you some extra credibility. People say, 'Oh, you have a master's so you must know something.' But you also have to understand mediation is not a typical career path where you go get a master's and then go get a job. Ultimately, you have to make your own career in this field."

Nova Southeastern University. One of the largest graduate programs in conflict resolution is at Nova Southeastern University, a private school in Fort Lauderdale, Florida. Through its Department of Conflict Analysis and Resolution, Nova offers both a Master of Science and a Ph.D. in dispute resolution. The school emphasizes practice skills and career preparation at least as much as theory. "The student will learn not only the philosophical basis for the practice of conflict resolution," explains Nova's recruiting materials, "but also the practical, specific tools of the trade."

For a Nova master's degree, tuition alone comes to just under $20,000 and for the Ph.D. about $45,000. Nova also offers a graduate certificate program—eight courses covering the fundamentals of conflict resolution—for about $10,000. To accommodate working adults who cannot relocate to the Florida campus for the two or three years it might take to complete a degree, Nova offers a distance learning format in which students can combine week-long limited residence at the school with on-line seminars and individualized studies.

George Mason, Antioch, and Nova are just a few of a large number of colleges and universities offering graduate programs in conflict resolution. Some of the other institutions include Columbia College in South Carolina, the University of Baltimore, Wayne State in Detroit, Teachers College at Columbia University, the University of Massachusetts at Boston, and the University of California at Los Angles (Metropolitan Studies Program). As noted earlier, the Program on Negotiation at Harvard Law School offers dispute resolution courses but not a degree. Several Quaker and Mennonite schools offer related programs in "peace studies." A comprehensive list produced by Nova University of more than seventy-five college and university programs (including those offering certificates) can be found at www.nova.edu/shss/DCAR.

So is it worth the time and tuition to get an advanced degree in dispute resolution? It depends.

Craig Coletta, coordinator for the National Association for Community Mediation, I think speaks for many midcareer mediators to whom advance degrees seem interesting but not essential. "I'm 32," says Coletta, "and probably of the last generation of mediators who all come from some other discipline." Before he became a mediator, Coletta had been an actor. Later he worked at the Pittsburgh Mediation Center for a man who had been an anthropologist. He continues:

> In my experience, it's what people bring from their other fields that enriches their work as mediators. When I worked at the Pittsburgh Mediation Center, for example, my boss's skills as an anthropologist taught me about narrative. I still use that skill a lot when I talk with the parties during mediation. It helps them process information.

But now, with the advent of school-based mediation and college degrees, you can literally start as a peer mediator in third grade and go on to get a bachelor's, master's, and doctorate. I know education is good, but I worry about people with no outside skills and professional experiences entering this field. [personal communication, July 2000]

The ACR takes a similar approach. On its Web site, in answer to the frequently asked question, "Should I get a college or graduate degree in dispute resolution?" the ACR responds,

Yes, if you understand that the more you learn, the better. However, there is no recognizable career path for mediators at present, as there is for other professions, and degrees in dispute resolution are a fairly recent development. The vast majority of professional mediators do not have such degrees, but have degrees in areas such as law, psychology, accounting, etc.

Personally, if I were choosing someone to mediate a case for me, I wouldn't favor a particular mediator simply because she had a degree, nor would I rate one lower because she lacked it. Nevertheless, depending on what your career goals may be, I can see situations where having a degree would be helpful.

Here's the best advice I can offer. If you are already in the mediation field, either as a practitioner or in a support capacity such as being a case manager at a mediation service, getting a degree to improve your theoretical knowledge and to learn advanced skills might enhance both your technique and marketability. Similarly, if you are in midcareer in a related field—human resources, for example—a conflict resolution degree might earn you a promotion. Certainly, if your aim is to teach, do research, or work for a domestic or international organization involved in conflict resolution, such as the Carter Center or the United Nations, then a degree makes perfect sense.

If you're just entering this field, however, I do not recommend starting with a degree. The money and time you'd spend on a college campus probably could be better spent getting some real-life experience. Take the basic training, do the apprenticeship, become a volunteer. If you find you like mediation and are good at it, develop your skills by handling real cases, either by starting your own practice or taking a position with a mediation service. (We'll talk more about specific job opportunities in Chapters Six and Seven.) Then maybe a few years down the road, if you want to enhance your theoretical understanding of conflict, develop new skills, and enhance your credibility with potential clients, picking up a degree—perhaps through a school that offers nonresidence, distance learning—might be worthwhile.

LICENSING AND CERTIFICATION

There is a lot of confusion about the terms *certification* and *licensing,* as they apply to mediators. Let's consider licensing first.

Licensing involves a government agency empowering a person to do something (such as practicing medicine or law) that they would otherwise be prohibited from doing. Presently, there is no licensing requirement for mediators. Some people advocate licensing mediators because they think it would help protect consumers against unqualified practitioners. Others oppose licensing, which would probably be based on test results or minimum educational requirements, because they say it would squeeze out of the field some of the most talented people who, though they may lack some required credential, have natural skills as mediators. The debate goes on. Eventually, some states probably will enact some sort of licensing requirement.

Certification is a bit more complicated. For example, I am a certified mediator, but what does that mean? It means only that I took a training program through my local community mediation center and that later the center issued a certificate attesting that I had successfully completed the program and am eligible to mediate cases there.

Increasing numbers of states and court systems now require the certification of mediators, but all certification means is that the mediator completed the training requirements and is qualified to handle cases referred through that state- or court-sponsored program. In North Carolina, for example, the Dispute Resolution Commission certifies mediators to handle civil cases, including divorce and family matters, filed in that state's courts. Mediators do not need to be certified if they have been selected directly by the parties, but judges may only appoint certified mediators. Similarly, some on-line dispute resolution services—Square Trade, for example, which handles many disputes generated by on-line auctions—now certify their mediators.

If, as a mediator, you want to receive cases referred through these types of programs and services, you'll need to get certified, but if all you want is to conduct a private mediation practice, you can hang out your shingle and not be concerned about certification.

I've encouraged you in this chapter to begin your mediation career with a simple, inexpensive basic training course at a community mediation center. It's a low-risk way of entering the field. Even so, basic training is a commitment of time and money, and there's no guarantee that once you complete the training you'll have either the opportunity or the desire to become an active mediator.

I still say take the training; it might be among the most valuable forty hours you spend in your life. The things you'll learn about how to listen and how to speak, about how to see problems from many points of view, and how to create solutions will benefit you, your friends, and your family throughout your life, even if you never sit at the head of a mediation table.

6

Job Opportunities in Mediation

A lbert Einstein spent the last thirty years of his life trying to formulate one equation that would explain everything in the universe—what he called a unified field theory. He never quite made it. Nevertheless, I've tried to construct my own unified field theory for the field of mediation. My goal was to create a single chart to depict all the major job opportunities in mediation. I didn't quite make it, either. As it turns out, it takes two charts: the one in this chapter and the one in the next.

In this chapter, we'll consider jobs that actually involve mediating. (In doing so, I'll refer to the same categories of mediation services discussed in Chapter Three, so if you're just dipping in here, you may want to pause and read Chapter Three first to understand the various services.) In the next chapter, we'll consider jobs in what I call mediation support.

IMPORTANT NOTE: START WITH WHAT YOU ALREADY KNOW

We spent considerable time in the previous chapter talking about an important rule for anyone thinking of becoming a media-

---

Note: All quotations in this chapter, unless otherwise noted, are based on interviews the author conducted during 1999 and 2000.

Table 6.1. Opportunities in Mediation

	Mediation Services				Independent Mediators in Private Practice		
	Community Centers Mediation	Court-Connected Programs	Government Programs	Private Dispute Resolution Companies	Divorce and Family Mediation	Other Specialty Practice	General Mediation Practice
Background	Varied	Law, social work, criminal justice, psychology	Law, labor relations, securities, human resources	Law, human resources, construction, accounting, psychology	Psychology, social work, law, parenting	Law, business, construction, human resources	Law, business, management
Full- or Part-Time	Part-time	Salaried positions in family mediation; other work mostly part-time	Full-time positions with FMCS and EEOC; most other is part-time contract work	Full-time if exclusive with national firm; most other is part-time panel work	Highest earners full-time and supplement with training; others part-time	Usually full-time needed to build adequate base of case referrals	Usually full-time needed to build adequate base of case referrals

Mediation Services				Independent Mediators in Private Practice		
Community Centers Mediation	Court-Connected Programs	Government Programs	Private Dispute Resolution Companies	Divorce and Family Mediation	Other Specialty Practice	General Mediation Practice
Training						
25 to 40 hours of basic training	For part-time work, often court-provided	Often agency-provided	Emphasis on experience, reputation more than training	40-hour ACR-approved course, plus supervision and mentoring	Basic and specialty training plus business skills	Basic training plus good business skills
Compensation						
$0 to $50 stipend; sometimes more for custody cases	$60K for salaried positions; $150 per hour; contract work; volunteer work	$80K salaried positions; $800 per case or $150 per hour; volunteer	$100K and up for busy panel members; $150 to $500 per hour for most	Average $100 per hour or $50K to $100K per year for full-time practice	Top gross $1 million; most bill $150 to $250 per hour and aim for $100K to $200K	Depends on case mix; low six figures or $100 to $250 per hour

tor: start by getting good-quality, basic training and then some experience, even as a volunteer.

Now that you're ready to look for a job or start your own practice, here's an important corollary to that earlier rule: take advantage of whatever background you already have. Although in theory a mediator with good practice skills can handle any type of case, in the real world, parties choose a mediator with knowledge of the subject matter in dispute. This is especially true when paying clients select one mediator from a roster. They want someone with relevant knowledge, for example, an understanding of insurance law, or manufacturing operations, or hospital administrative procedures.

Therefore, position yourself in the mediation field by taking advantage of whatever professional, work, or personal background you already have that will appeal to a particular type of disputant. If you are a nurse, consider specializing in mediating medical-related disputes. Even a hobby, such as remodeling, can offer a specialty in residential construction. Parenting, too, can offer an appealing background for a practice in divorce, family, or school-based mediation.

My point is not that you should stay locked as a specialist in whatever field you've recently been engaged, only that when starting out, you will increase your marketability by taking advantage of what you already know.

COMMUNITY MEDIATION CENTERS

The five to six hundred nonprofit community mediation centers around the country rely almost exclusively on volunteer mediators. People are willing to volunteer, as I've noted, partly because community mediation centers offer low-cost, basic mediator training and the opportunity to mediate a variety of interesting cases.

A few centers pay their mediators a small stipend, maybe $25 per case. Centers that accept child custody cases on referral from the local family court might pay mediators with special training in this area a higher stipend, maybe $100 a case. I know of one center that pays $50 to arbitrators in small commercial cases. I know other centers that pay none of their mediators anything; you're lucky to get your parking ticket stamped.

Nevertheless, don't overlook volunteering at a community mediation center as a good way to start networking your way into the field—and toward a paying job.

"People get jobs because their skills become known to their colleagues," advises Craig Coletta, coordinator for the National Association for Community Mediation. "One of the best ways to get a job in the mediation field is to volunteer at a community mediation center in your area and meet other people working in the field." Community mediation centers are also good places to find entry-level positions in mediation support, a topic we'll examine further in Chapter Seven.

To find a community mediation center where you live, check the phone directory under "mediation" or visit the National Association for Community Mediation's Web site (www.nafcm.org), where you will find contact information for hundreds of centers nationwide.

COURT-CONNECTED MEDIATION PROGRAMS

Trial courts in most states have set up mediation programs to try to resolve civil (noncriminal) cases, such as those involving contracts, consumer claims, personal injuries, and divorces. Typically, people filing lawsuits are either required or strongly encouraged to try mediation before continuing with their case. In Florida, for example, trial judges have discretion to order people to mediation. If they do, the parties have to show up for at least one session.

The best-paying mediator jobs in state-connected programs are those in states that employ their own full-time, salaried mediators to handle divorce cases. In these states, mediation for divorcing couples tends to be mandatory, at least for issues such as custody and visitation that affect children. California is the leading state in this regard. Mediators employed by the California court program often have master's degrees in the social sciences and professional backgrounds in mental health or family counseling. Advanced mediator training is usually provided by the court. Full-time positions carry salaries ranging from about $45,000 to $65,000.

The following is excerpted from a job notice for a full-time mediator with the court program in Santa Barbara County, California.

SUPERIOR COURT
STATE OF CALIFORNIA—
COUNTY OF SANTA BARBARA

Title: Family Custody Mediator/Evaluator

Salary: $40,591–49,552 per year; full-time position with benefits

Duties: Supports the court process by investigating and mediating referrals from Superior Court judges regarding civil custody of minors and visitation rights; mediates with parents to arrive at mutually acceptable resolutions in the best interest of the children.

Background: Master's degree in psychology, social work, family and child counseling or related area, and at least two years' experience in counseling or psychotherapy

---

Full-time salaried positions like the one from California are more the exception than the rule. Court-connected programs in most states offer only part-time work, and compensation varies by state and even by county, as well as by case type.

Some states pay mediators nothing (but may pick up your parking and other expenses); others pay reasonably well. In Florida, for example, contract mediators appointed by the court to handle divorce cases receive $125 an hour from the court when the family cannot pay; when parties select their own mediator, compensation is whatever the market will bear, with some mediators earning $250 an hour. In contrast, mediator pay in the Virginia court program ranges from only $80 for a civil case (nondivorce) to $200 for a full divorce case.

In most states, if you want the courts to refer cases to you as a mediator, you have to become certified to work in their program. Usually that means showing that you have adequate training and experience, but you may be required to complete a special court-approved training program. These are sometimes provided by the court itself or by the local community mediation center. (In some states, parties are free to choose a noncertified mediator if they wish.)

Training requirements also vary, depending on the type of cases to be mediated and sometimes on the educational and professional background of the trainee.

For example, in Oregon you don't need any particular educational background to mediate civil (nondivorce) cases, but you do need to complete thirty hours of basic mediation training plus six hours of training about the court system. To mediate child-related issues in a divorce case, however, you need a master's degree in a behavioral science or a law degree, and you must complete thirty hours of mediation training, twenty-four hours of domestic relations training, graduate-level work in child development, domestic violence, and substance abuse, twenty supervised mediations, and twelve hours of continuing education each year. To mediate financial issues in a divorce case, the requirements are even more stringent, including a master's or law degree and more than one hundred hours of training.

Be aware that some states require mediators working in court-connected programs to be lawyers. In Florida, for example, where more than five thousand certified mediators handle civil cases in the court-connected program, nonlawyers can only handle cases under $15,000 in value; all the larger cases are reserved for lawyer-mediators.

Other states permit nonlawyers to mediate but may require they take additional training. In North Carolina, for example, certification is available to lawyers as well as nonlawyers, but nonlawyers must complete an additional six hours of training on court procedures and common legal issues arising in civil cases; they must also provide letters of reference as to their good character, among other requirements.

Mediators, once they have been certified for court programs, typically put their names on a list, and either the court assigns them cases on a rotating basis or the parties choose a mediator from the list. It can sometimes be tough for nonlawyer mediators to get chosen. Even if the parties themselves don't care whether the mediator is a lawyer or not, their attorneys often do and steer them toward selecting one. The frustration this can cause is reflected in a recent Internet posting:

> I live in Austin, Texas, have an M.B.A., have completed my required mediation education and training, but have found that work as a mediator, other than nonpaid volunteer mediation, is hard to come by. The problem seems to be that attorneys have cornered the market in this city. Potential clients get the names of mediators from their attorneys or judges, and it appears they generally refer their clients to other attorneys who mediate. [notice posted on mediate.com, 11/28/00]

Where the parties or judges are free to select whatever mediator they want from a court's roster, a small number of popular mediators tend to be picked frequently, and the rest hear relatively few cases. In Virginia, where about four thousand cases are mediated annually, a program administrator estimates 25 percent of the state's one thousand certified mediators hear most of the cases; in Florida, an administrator says that probably 10 percent of the state's five thousand mediators do 90 percent of the work.

Even where compensation is slight and the work only occasional, I still encourage aspiring mediators to participate in court-connected programs. They offer another opportunity to develop skills, to meet other professionals, and get the word out in the community that you are available as a mediator.

To learn whether your state has a court-connected mediation program and, if so, what the educational and training requirements and compensation are, contact the clerk of the local trial court (often called a district court) in your community. Alternatively, contact the National Center on State Courts in Williamsburg, Virginia, which maintains information about court-connected mediation programs in all the states. Call the center at (800) 616–6164 or visit their Web site: www.ncsc.dni.us. Go to the section, "Knowledge Management Office," and follow the links to "Alternative Dispute Resolution."

GOVERNMENT MEDIATION PROGRAMS

Many departments and agencies of the federal government have in the past decade become significant employers of mediators. This is due in part to laws such as the Administrative Dispute Resolution Act of 1996 that require or encourage governmental use of ADR.

In 1998, for example, an Interagency ADR Working Group was established by presidential directive within the U.S. Department of Justice to promote greater use of mediation among all federal departments and agencies. Each must report annually on its use of mediation and other forms of alternative dispute resolution. As an example, the U.S. Department of Agriculture reported in a recent year that its ADR budget was $2.8 million; it had thirty full-time employees involved in ADR, including program managers and mediators, and the primary focus was on resolving workplace disputes within the agency. For a list of ADR coordinators at each federal department and agency, including contact information, visit the U.S. Department of Justice Web site at www.usdoj.gov/odr and follow the prompts to "Interagency Working Group" and then to "Federal Agency ADR Contacts."

The U.S. government's official Web site for employment information is usajobs.opm.gov. The site, maintained by the Office of Personnel Management, posts vacancy listings for all federal agencies and provides detailed information on how to apply for jobs. To find openings for mediators on this Web site, try searching under "mediator," "conciliation specialist," or "alternative dispute resolution."

In the rest of this section, we'll look at some of the agencies that are most active in hiring or contracting with mediators to handle cases arising under federal programs.

Federal Mediation and Conciliation Service

Created by Congress in 1947 as an independent agency to promote stable labor-management relations, the Federal Mediation and Conciliation Service (FMCS) mediates contract disputes between employers and unions in the private and government sectors. The FMCS also mediates disputes within government agencies and between agencies and the public; it trains personnel at other agencies to set up their own dispute resolution systems.

Currently, the FMCS employs about 120 full-time mediators who work either at the agency's Washington, D.C. headquarters or at field offices throughout the country. Mediators handle labor cases but may also be "loaned" to other federal agencies to handle cases of other types, such as internal claims of employment discrimination.

The excerpted notice to follow shows salary and qualification requirements typical for these types of mediator positions. The initials GS, for Government Service, are part of the standard designation for pay scales in federal government jobs.

FEDERAL MEDIATION AND CONCILIATION SERVICE
2100 K St., N.W., Washington, DC 20427

Title: Mediator

Salary: Starting GS-12 ($44,953–$47,831); potential to GS-14 ($63,169–$87,377)

Qualifications: Substantial full-time experience acquired over a period of several years in the negotiation of collective bargaining agreements. Candidates who fall short of these requirements may be considered for developmental positions at the GS-9 or GS-11 levels at the agency's larger field offices, where mentoring with an experienced mediator is available.

For more information about job opportunities at the FMCS, contact the agency at its Washington, D.C. headquarters at (202) 606-8100 or its Web site: www.fmcs.gov.

EQUAL EMPLOYMENT OPPORTUNITY COMMISSION

The EEOC enforces Title VII of the Civil Rights Act of 1964, which prohibits workplace discrimination based on race, sex, national origin, color, or religion. The EEOC also enforces the Equal Pay Act, the Age Discrimination in Employment Act, and the Americans with Disabilities Act.

As an alternative to its normal investigative and litigation process, the EEOC began experimenting with mediation in 1991 and, based on successful results, launched the program nationally in 1999. In the year 2000, the mediation program received nearly

$13 million in funds and was operational in all of the agency's district offices, each of which has its own mediation coordinator. Nearly five thousand workplace discrimination cases were mediated.

EEOC's mediation program is administered primarily through its twenty-five district offices, which together employ some ninety-two mediators. This number includes the twenty-five ADR coordinators at each district office, plus sixty-seven full-time "internal" mediators distributed among the offices. EEOC offices also contract with outside mediators who are trained in both mediation and the laws enforced by the agency.

In the Cleveland District Office, for example, ADR coordinator Loretta Feller oversees the work of two full-time staff mediators plus another who works in the agency's Cincinnati office. Minimum qualifications for an EEOC staff mediator generally include five years of experience in negotiation and facilitation and three to five years working with EEOC, including one year of mediation experience. In the Cleveland office, all three internal mediators have backgrounds as EEOC investigators or managers and were subsequently trained by the agency in mediation. They generally mediate two to three cases per week and spend the rest of their time doing scheduling and other administrative work related to the cases. Their salaries range from $62,000 to $81,000 per year.

The Cleveland office also maintains a roster of some forty-five external mediators throughout Ohio. These mediators were recruited based on their backgrounds in employment discrimination law and their training and experience as mediators. About three-fourths are attorneys, and the rest are either involved in human resources or work full-time as mediators. Feller prefers to have cases handled by her internal mediators, but when they are not available because of geography, workload, or conflicts of interest, she selects external mediators from the roster on a rotating basis. Most are selected just two or three times a year. In some years, the external mediators serve as volunteers when there is no funding available, but in other years they are paid. A few EEOC district offices, including Seattle and San Francisco, recently have had funds to pay external mediators at a rate of $800 per case. For a profile of one external mediator who works through the San Francisco office, see Chapter Three.

Other government agencies have established internal programs to resolve workplace discrimination claims so that the claims do not have to be referred out to the EEOC. For example, the U.S. Postal Service has set up an internal mediation system called REDRESS (Resolve Employee Disputes, Reach Equitable Solutions Swiftly). In one recent year, more than thirteen thousand cases were successfully mediated. To handle this volume of cases, the postal service primarily depends on outside, nonpostal mediators who work for the program under contract. To become certified by the agency to mediate these cases, prospective mediators take REDRESS-sponsored training. Already thirty-five hundred mediators have been put on the postal service's mediation roster; at this writing, the agency had closed the list and was not accepting new names. For more information on this program and to learn if the agency is accepting new mediators, contact the national REDRESS office at (202) 268–3991.

OTHER AGENCIES

Other full-time mediator jobs are scattered throughout the federal bureaucracy. Those with well-established mediation programs include

National Mediation Board. This agency, which works to avert strikes involving railroads, airlines, and other forms of transportation, employs full-time mediators. A recent job posting for a mediator quoted a salary range of $51,204–$93,537. For more information, contact the agency at its headquarters: 1301 K St., N.W., Washington, DC 20572.

Community Relations Service. This agency, part of the U.S. Department of Justice, helps local communities resolve racial and ethnic conflicts. Staff trained in mediation are stationed in ten regional and four field offices across the country and available on a twenty-four-hour basis. For more information, visit the agency's Web site: www.usdoj.gov/crs.

National Association of Securities Dealers (NASD). NASD is a private corporation regulated by the Securities and Exchange Commission (SEC) and for our purposes can be grouped with other government agencies. To help resolve disputes between investors and their brokerage firms, NASD has set up what it deems the largest dispute resolution forum in the securities industry.

No specific experience in the securities industry is required in order to be included on NASD's nationwide roster of approved mediators, but a knowledge of the laws and practices of the industry make it more likely a mediator will be selected by the parties. Mediators are paid directly by the parties at a rate of $150 per hour (or higher if the parties agree) plus expenses. Currently, NASD is looking to expand mediator panels in twenty cities, including Albany and Buffalo, New York, Kansas City, Missouri, Omaha, Nebraska, San Diego, California, and Washington, District of Columbia. For more information, contact NASD Regulation, Inc., Mediation Director, 125 Broad Street, 36th Floor, New York, NY 10004; (212) 858–3915; Web site: www.nasdadr.com.

STATE GOVERNMENT PROGRAMS

Programs run by state governments may also offer mediators opportunities for full-time, part-time, or contract employment.

In Massachusetts, the State Department of Education employs mediators to handle disputes concerning special education programs, and the Office of the Attorney General runs a program involving peer mediation in the schools. A statewide Office of Dispute Resolution maintains a panel of some sixty mediators, mostly private practitioners, who have contracts with other state agencies to hear cases involving housing, land use, state policy, and other matters.

In Oregon, a new state commission is training mediators to handle disputes involving people with disabilities. If planned funding is available, the mediators will be paid between $50 and $200 an hour. The Oregon Commission on Dispute Resolution coordinates ADR programs throughout the state and maintains a roster of mediators in the private sector who are available to serve in state-run mediation programs.

As in Massachusetts and Oregon, most states now have, or are in the process of forming, special offices to coordinate mediation services throughout the state. Some offices are sponsored or partly funded by state governments; others are independent, nonprofit organizations that assume this role themselves. A good way to learn about job opportunities in your state is by contacting the statewide mediation office. A list of these offices appears in Resource C.

PRIVATE DISPUTE RESOLUTION COMPANIES

Private companies providing alternative dispute resolution services offer various job opportunities for mediators. At the high end, if you're an experienced mediator, particularly with a legal background, you can become an active, independent contractor with a large, national ADR firm. At the lower end, you can join the panel of a smaller, local ADR firm and hope they do enough business to call you once in a while to hear a case. In addition, on-line dispute resolution firms are now signing up mediators to help resolve a growing volume of commercial disputes on the Web. In this section, we'll consider job opportunities at each of these types of private mediation services.

JAMS

The largest private, for-profit ADR firm today remains JAMS (formerly Judicial Arbitration & Mediation Services), headquartered in Irvine, California. For many years, the company had been owned by venture capitalists and private investors, but in 1999 a group of forty-four JAMS mediators and the firm's chief executive officer bought the company themselves; today it is the only national mediation company owned by the mediators.

JAMS aims for the market segment that includes large-dollar commercial disputes. "JAMS is known for high-stakes, multiparty and complex cases, and its mediators are the cream of the crop," notes JAMS vice president for marketing, Deana Kardel. She reports that in a recent year the company handled nearly thirteen thousand cases in its twenty-some offices throughout the country and generated revenue of about $55 million.

About 60 percent of JAMS' two hundred neutrals are retired judges, and the other 40 percent are attorneys, most of them retired. There are no business people or academics on the panel, although the company has recently signed up a former U.S. ambassador as an international mediator.

JAMS mediators are all exclusive with the company—they work for no other ADR firms—and are paid according to the business they bring in. Their time is charged to the parties at rates of $350 an hour and higher. Depending on how in demand they are as mediators and how complex their cases are, most JAMS mediators earn from $150,000 to more than $1 million a year, making them among the highest-paid mediators in the country.

JAMS can be reached at its Irvine corporate headquarters at (949) 224-JAMS or at its Web site: www.jamsadr.com.

American Arbitration Association

The American Arbitration Association (AAA), begun more than seventy-five years ago, has expanded beyond its middle name to include, among its services, mediation. Although it handles many of the same types of complex, commercial cases as JAMS and other for-profit ADR firms, AAA also focuses on education and maintains a not-for-profit status. AAA has the competitive advantage of being written into thousands of employment, insurance, construction, and general commercial contracts as the ADR provider of choice. As a result, AAA's caseload is massive: 198,000 cases in a recent year.

AAA operates thirty-seven offices domestically and one in Dublin, Ireland. The organization has about twelve thousand neutrals on its panels, about one thousand of whom are mediators; the rest do arbitration. "Mediation is something you have to do frequently to stay good at it," explains AAA senior vice president Mark Appel, "so we're selective about who gets on our mediation panel." Some of the mediators practice other professions, such as law, and mediate for AAA only occasionally, but many others are full-time mediators who handle a large volume of cases. Unlike JAMS, AAA does not have exclusive arrangements with its neutrals.

AAA mediators set their own fees, which range from about $125 an hour for less experienced mediators handling smaller cases to about $500 an hour for highly skilled, commercial mediators handling seven-figure disputes. AAA's highest-paid mediator charges $7,500 a day. "It's a lot of money," comments Appel, "but people believe this mediator is worth it."

Most AAA mediators are lawyers, but there are nonlawyers on the panel, too. "Nonlawyer mediators," says Appel, "are likely to come from the industry that uses their services." For example, engineers, architects, contractors, or construction managers may mediate disputes in the construction industry. Accountants often mediate general commercial cases. "In the employment setting, we have folks from HR, or people who come from labor relations," says Appel.

How do you get to be an AAA mediator? "First, get yourself trained," advises Appel. He continues:

> Then I'd recommend you sign on with a no-pay or low-pay community or court-connected program to cut your teeth and get some actual experience. You should also begin learning from us. Become a member of AAA, get our literature, look at our Web site, read about the field. Then start soliciting opportunities to serve as mediator

with people who respect your judgment. Once you have a track record, then come to us and apply to be on our roster. Generally, we'll want to see that you've done ten to twenty business-to-business or employment cases. Community cases and family disputes won't qualify you.

"Officially, applicants for AAA's mediation panel should have ten years experience, but exceptions can be made," says Appel. "More important than ten years is a track record of success as a mediator. We're not looking for people just out of school, but high-quality mediation experience is more important to us than an arbitrary number of years."

Appel continues,

Once you apply to be on the panel, our regional office closest to where you live will check your references, speak to parties whose cases you mediated, and run your name past our local advisory group to vet your qualifications. If you're added to our roster, you become part of our national panel and are eligible for continuing education, which we offer every six months. We want our mediators to grow with us.

For more information about the AAA, contact the corporate headquarters in New York City at (800) 778–7879, or visit their Web site: www.adr.org. For names and contact information for other national ADR firms, see Resource D.

Now let's look at job opportunities with a smaller ADR firm—one that doesn't often compete head-on with JAMS or AAA but has developed a market within its own region.

Massachusetts Dispute Resolution Services

Founded in 1993 by a former litigating attorney, this for-profit, private ADR firm handles matters such as personal injury claims, employment disputes, real estate, construction, and divorce. The firm has its main offices in Salem and Boston and has conference space available in executive office suites throughout the state. Cases are heard by Brian R. Jerome, the company's founder and sole owner, and a panel of forty mediators and arbitrators.

MDRS panel members, after splitting fees with the company, earn about $100 per hour for both commercial and divorce cases. Annual earnings of individual mediators and arbitrators who work with the company range from $500 to $20,000 for the most active panel member.

All members of the MDRS panel are either retired judges or experienced attorneys. Of the three mediators who handle the firm's divorces, one is a full-time mediator who used to practice law, and the other two are part-time mediators who still keep up their law practice.

That all the members of the MRDS panel are lawyers may be disconcerting to nonlawyers, but it is typical of what you find in the smaller regional firms handling this type of caseload. Explains owner Jerome, "How does one become a mediator for my firm? I'm afraid the answer is: you become a lawyer, practice for about fifteen years, then give me a call. Or you became a judge and retire from the bench." Jerome continues:

> Nonlawyers may not want to hear this, but if you're in the private ADR business and you want to be hired, you've got to offer your customers something they want, and the types of cases pending in the courts that have value are the ones that are going to experienced neutrals (mediators and arbitrators) who are also knowledgeable in the law.
>
> That's not to say nonlawyers can't be great mediators, but our firm is focused on a strata of cases that are looking for retired judges or gray-haired, experienced attorney-neutrals. And it's firms like ours that are making a reasonable living doing mediation and arbitration on a full-time basis.

Lest this be too distressing to nonlawyer readers, bear in mind that, as I noted earlier, the largest national ADR organization, AAA, with twelve thousand neutrals, does use nonlawyers as mediators, including engineers, architects, building contractors, and construction managers. There are also smaller private ADR firms with nonlawyer mediators on their panels. I know this from personal experience. The company I founded, Empire Mediation & Arbitration, Inc., has used nonlawyer mediators.

I recall one large, complex construction case in which we provided the six different parties a co-mediation team consisting of a lawyer with extensive experience in construction litigation and a recently retired civil engineer who had taken mediator training. That combination turned out to be perfect. The more than $2 million claims involved were settled to the satisfaction of all six parties after eleven hours of mediation. In another case involving claims against a contractor for a faulty wooden deck built on the back of a residential home, we provided a home builder who had experience building decks as the mediator, and that case also settled. In other cases, we have been able to use mediators with backgrounds in nursing, teaching, and auto repair.

ON-LINE DISPUTE RESOLUTION

Jupiter Research, a firm that analyzes business trends on the Internet, recently surveyed business-to-business e-commerce sites and found a majority have no policy regarding conflict resolution. In a report titled "Conflict Resolution: Rising Above the Oncoming Flood," Jupiter concludes: "For Net Markets to develop trust between buyers and sellers, they must work quickly to formulate clear mediation policies."

Currently, fees paid to mediators by on-line mediation services are modest compared with those paid for regular face-to-face mediation by regular private ADR providers. Yet as the volume of Internet transactions and disputes continues to increase, my guess is that on-line mediation will become significantly more lucrative. Furthermore, on-line mediation is not only for disputes that originate on-line, such as those involving auctions, but many other types of disputes, such as insurance claims or business matters, where for one reason or another the parties are not able to meet face-to-face.

Accordingly, this is an excellent time for a new mediator to sign up with the on-line services and develop skills and credentials in on-line mediation. Those who begin now will in five years be considered experts at on-line mediation and be able to command whatever the highest fees are at that time.

Furthermore, because on-line disputes tend to concern straightforward commercial transactions rather than complex legal cases, on-line mediation firms do not appear to favor mediators with law backgrounds to the same extent as other private ADR companies. In short, there appears to be more opportunity for nonlawyer mediators on-line.

A good place to begin a search for mediation opportunities on-line is Mediate.com, an on-line resource for both mediators and potential clients. This site offers referrals and directories, maintains an excellent library of resources (Mediation Information and Resource Centers), and develops Web sites and Internet technology for practitioners and organizations.

Jim Melamed, cofounder and chief executive officer of Mediate.com, concurs that mediators who are serious about their practice need to embrace on-line mediation as a component of their practice. Melamed advises:

> In the future, we won't talk so much in terms of face-to-face mediation or of on-line mediation but of our ability as mediators to best integrate the Internet into our practices. For example, if I'm doing divorce mediation, I can meet with a couple face-to-face several times, but later I can also work with them on-line at lower cost. Similarly, if I'm mediating a communitywide dispute, I can have an on-line discussion with literally hundreds of participants.

I encourage people getting into this field to learn how to conduct on-line mediation and facilitation as a way to distinguish themselves from other "run-of-the-mill" mediator wannabes.

Following are brief sketches of a few on-line mediation services and the opportunities they currently offer mediators.

Online Resolution

Online Resolution, a service that was spun off from Mediate.com in 2000, offers mediation of all kinds of disputes, from e-commerce to family issues.

Mediators are accepted onto the panel based on training and experience. Online Resolution offers some free community mediation services, and less experienced mediators are encouraged to handle these cases on a volunteer basis. More experienced mediators are invited to mediate larger, commercial cases and are paid between $50 and $100 per hour.

A service of special interest to mediators in private practice is Online Resolution's "Resolution Rooms"—on-line environments that anyone can buy in order to conduct an on-line mediation. The "rooms," customized with the mediator's own logo, are password-protected and equipped with text, image, and audio, as well as e-mail, a polling mechanism, instant messaging, document sharing, threaded discussions, and a space for private caucus that is open only to the neutral and to one party at a time. Mediators can buy one room or clusters of up to twenty rooms at a discount.

To apply to join Online Resolution's mediation panel, contact the company at their Web site: onlineresolution.com.

Square Trade

This firm specializes in resolving disputes arising out of on-line transactions, such as nondelivery of goods or services, misrepresentation, improper selling practices, guarantees or warranties that aren't honored, unsatisfactory services, credit and billing problems, and unfulfilled contracts. Square Trade got its start handling disputes from E-bay, the on-line auction site, and continues to mediate a significant number of auction-related matters. In a recent year, Square Trade is said to have handled more than thirty-thousand cases, with an 80 percent-plus settlement rate.

When a dispute is filed, the parties are encouraged to resolve it themselves through direct negotiation, discussing the issues through a password-protected Case Page on the SquareTrade Web site. If that effort fails, the parties may request a mediator.

Square Trade mediators are paid $30 per case for simple, low-value auction disputes ($200–300 in dispute is typical) and higher amounts for other types of cases, scaled to the value in dispute.

Currently, Square Trade has about three hundred mediators. In recruiting mediators, the firm looks at experience levels, especially in regard to

- Specialty areas of e-commerce, such as intellectual property, employment and service matters, real estate and construction, and general commercial disputes

- International experience as a neutral

- Multilingual skills or cross-cultural expertise

Note that a legal background is not among the listed factors for recruiting mediators.

Square Trade offers an additional training program to help mediators translate off-line mediation skills into on-line skills. The training is free of charge, but in exchange Square Trade will require you to sign a noncompete clause barring you from working with another on-line company while working with Square Trade and for six months afterward.

Mediators who complete the training and are accepted onto the Square Trade panel are assigned five cases initially and then evaluated. Following successful evaluation, they receive certification as a Square Trade mediator.

For more information on being a Square Trade mediator, visit the firm's Web site: www.squaretrade.com.

eResolution

This service specializes in international e-business disputes. It is best known for providing domain name dispute resolution for ICANN (Internet Corporation for Assigned Names and Numbers), a group that controls the "real estate" of the Internet. To date, eResolution reports it has resolved some two hundred domain name disputes.

Given the global reach of its business and its emphasis on complex international commercial disputes, it is not surprising that eResolution's panels of mediators consist mostly of attorneys, academics, and business people.

To learn more about eResolution and opportunities to join its mediation panels, contact the firm at their Web site: www.eresolution.com.

Cybersettle

This service, which is well funded and has received considerable publicity, uses a computer-assisted method of blind bidding to settle insurance claims. Each side to a dispute makes an offer to settle. If the two sides come within a predetermined percentage of each other (typically 30 percent), the computer will split the difference and declare a settlement. There are no human mediators involved, so job opportunities at Cybersettle.com and with competitive on-line services such as Clicknsettle.com are only in sales and support. (For more on opportunities in mediation support, see Chapter Seven.)

INDEPENDENT MEDIATORS IN PRIVATE PRACTICE

Having a private mediation practice is many people's dream; it's what they imagined when they first thought of getting into the field. Establishing a private practice is a difficult path but an extraordinarily rewarding one if you can travel it successfully.

Unfortunately, there are no "job opening" notices to help you get started. At some point, after getting proper training and some experience, you will just have to hang out your shingle and go for it. That means renting an office or setting up one in your home, printing stationery and business cards, getting phone and fax lines and probably a Web site, opening a bank account, buying insurance, and attending to all the other details involved in starting a business.

And then you'll need cases. "In the private sector, one basically gets or doesn't get cases based on one's reputation as a mediator," says Jim Melamed, who, as cofounder of Mediate.com, advises many people looking to start their own practice. "No one is going to hand you anything on a silver platter—you're going to have to earn it the old-fashioned way."

Melamed says he used to think two years was a reasonable period of time in which to start a mediation practice and at least break even. "But I've come lately to believe the necessary time may be longer," he says. "This may be because there are more and more mediators out there, so you have to work harder to differentiate yourself in the marketplace."

He continues:

> Sure, a well-known judge who retires and sets up as a mediator may have a shorter time-frame, but others may take several years to establish themselves. Then there are those with no professional background or no personal charisma or no entrepreneurial spirit, and basically they will never be successful.
>
> In the private sector, you really do need to be an entrepreneur. It's one of the paradoxes of this field, because we talk collaboration, but unless you have good business instincts, you're not going to get the cases. For example, I used to advise if someone calls you have to get back to them the same day, but now I think you've got to return the call as soon as possible. It's that competitive.

Melamed advises those launching private practices to continue their education and establish relationships with colleagues by joining professional organizations like the Association for Conflict Resolution—a national group formed by the merger of the Academy of Family Mediators, the Society of Professionals in Dispute Resolution, and the Conflict Resolution Education Network (CREnet). Lawyer-mediators can join the American Bar Association's Section on Dispute Resolution. "You need to get networked within the ADR community so other practitioners know you," he says. "Write articles, make presentations at conventions, let other mediators come to know your dedication, capacity, intelligence, and commitment to the field. That's where many of your referrals will come from."

While you're waiting for your practice to develop, you can also pick up some extra experience and income by handling cases through local court-connected or government mediation programs, and through regional or national ADR firms that will accept you onto their panels.

"You've got to rub shoulders with the people who refer cases, so you've got to think about who are the referral sources for the kind of practice you're developing," Melamed advises.

> If you're thinking of developing a practice in workplace mediation, realize it's not the employees or the company president who will want to bring in a mediator, it's the upper-level management and maybe the human resource director. In divorce mediation, you need to reach all the mental health professionals, accountants, and of course divorce lawyers, but also barbers and beauticians—these people know what's happening in their customers' lives, and can steer them toward mediation.
>
> Finally, you'd be a fool not to take advantage of your entire history of contacts and your personal network. If you were in software development and now want to go into divorce mediation, fine, but you still need to con-

tact all the software people you know to let them know about your new line of work.

As I noted in Chapter Three, mediators in private practice generally engage in one of three types of work: divorce and family mediation, a specialty other than divorce, or general practice. We'll consider each of these next.

DIVORCE AND FAMILY MEDIATION

Most mediators who engage in independent, private practice do so as divorce mediators. This is because there is a strong and growing demand for divorce mediation—in some cities upwards of 25 percent of divorcing couples choose to mediate—and also because one can build a practice by cultivating a fairly narrow range of referral sources, principally therapists, clergy, and divorce attorneys.

What fees you can command as a divorce mediator will vary with the size of the community where you practice and the part of the market you reach. In a large city, mediators catering mostly to affluent couples may charge $200 an hour or more. One mediator in California, whose clientele includes movie stars and media executives, charges $500 an hour. In small towns or rural communities, mediators may be happy to get $50 an hour. Overall, divorce mediators in midsize communities can expect to earn on average about $100 to $150 an hour; those who offer a sliding fee scale, based on ability to pay, generally will accept around $60 to $75 an hour.

Although some divorce mediators may be earning sizable six-figure incomes, I think a fair estimate of what full-time mediators make in average-size cities is $50,000 to $100,000 per year. It's worth noting, however, that many active divorce mediators do not mediate full-time. Most do some training of new mediators on the side or continue to practice on a reduced basis whatever profession that were in before they became mediators. Thus some continue a therapy practice; others keep up their law practice.

You may wonder if there is enough demand for divorce mediation in your community to support another mediator. A glance at your local Yellow Pages may reveal a lengthy list of people who have opened practices as divorce mediators. I wouldn't worry about it. My guess is that half or more of those listed don't mediate ten cases a year. That's not because the market is saturated but because the ones who aren't busy are either just dabbling in mediation while spending most of their time doing something else or they just don't have the skills, personality, or ambition to build a successful practice. The handful of mediators who are making a living at mediation probably do 75 percent of the work in town. They're the ones who have learned how to market themselves. Where I live, most divorce mediators listed in the phone book handle few if any cases, whereas the mediator who is most in demand has a two-month waiting list for new clients.

If you're serious about becoming a divorce mediator and are willing to invest the time and energy to develop a practice, there's no reason you can't join the group of successful mediators in your community, as Dolly Hinkley did. Hinkley became a divorce mediator in 1984, when the field was still very young. A divorced mother of four, she was employed as property manager at a senior citizen's high-rise in Rochester, New York. For several years, with her employer's permission, she worked that job until 1:00 P.M., then mediated in the afternoons. She kept both occupations going for ten years.

She recalls, "It was an uphill struggle in those days because of resistance from the Bar Association, but I did a lot of networking with mental health professionals and attorneys, and took a lot of people out to lunch so they'd get to know me and my practice" (personal communication, February 2001). She gave presentations to many interest groups, such as Equal Rights for Fathers and the American Association of University Women.

Today Hinkley has one of the better-established divorce mediation practices in Rochester. She works out of her home in the suburbs, and most of her referrals come from former clients. She continues, however, to network with referral sources and regularly accepts invitations to speak before support groups of people going through separation and divorce.

Her fees, from $75 to $130 an hour, are on a sliding scale, based on a couple's income. Each year she completes between forty and fifty mediations. Some couples do not complete mediation, she explains, because they either reconcile or get lazy and drag out or postpone the process. In addition to divorce, Hinkley does some marriage mediation such as prenuptial mediation and helping married couples with specific issues; she also mediates disputes among family members and does volunteer mediation at the local community mediation center.

Hinkley estimates that she has about twenty billable hours a week. "Mediating full-time doesn't mean you're mediating nine to five every day," she explains, noting that although she charges for drafting documents, she generally doesn't bill for the time she spends preparing for each session. "For example," she says, "if I know a couple is going to be talking about a particular company's retirement plan, I do some research in my files about that plan to refresh my memory of it. Or if they have a particular type of IRA—Roth, or whatever, I find out what's the latest on that plan in terms of new laws or court decisions."

I asked Hinkley how she feels about competition from so many new people getting trained in mediation. "At first I thought there was only a finite pie to divide up among mediators," she says, "but the demand for divorce mediation keeps increasing. It's not that the number of divorces is increasing, but more people getting divorced are now looking at mediation first rather than going to attorneys. Years ago, in support groups people used to ask each other, 'Who's your lawyer?' but now it's 'Who's your mediator?'"

Hinkley says she's glad to help new people coming into the field. "I'll help anybody who really wants to be a mediator," she says, "but when I get an initial call from somebody, I don't encourage them because I know it takes a considerable amount of time to get set up and build a profitable practice. Most don't want to give up their day job, but I know from my own experience that it's only when you do quit the day job and put all your energies into mediation that you can become successful. If the person who calls me has already made that decision—to be serious about building a practice—then I'll help them."

Burn-out affects most mediators, but probably none more than those doing divorce. "Sure, I get burned out," says Hinkley. "Some couples—or one person in a couple—can give me instant burn-out. I take a lot of vacations. I've been to almost eighty different countries. I find I really need to travel three times a year and also take a lot of long weekends."

But Hinkley can also suffer from what she calls anti-burn-out.

> During this past December, lots of my clients were postponing sessions until after the holidays, so I had a lot of free time. I was bored to death. One day I even went to the movies by myself. Finally, I couldn't stand it. I couldn't wait until the next client. I missed mediating.
>
> I've met some really nice people from doing this work, people who are really concerned about their children and who want to do best for their spouse. I'd rather a couple stay together if possible, but if they're going to separate, I'd rather they do it in a cooperative rather than adversarial way, and I like being the one to help them. I don't think I'm ever going to retire.

There are plenty of resources available to help you get started with a divorce mediation practice. Recall our discussion in the previous chapter about selecting a divorce mediation trainer approved by the Association for Conflict Resolution and about how many trainers will help you get started by mentoring you, introducing you to referral sources, and providing forms to use in your practice.

You can also purchase forms and other materials, such as computer programs for case tracking, from private vendors, many of whom advertise in publications and on Web sites of the major mediation organizations, such as Mediate.com, and the ACR. The ACR itself sells for less than $150 a "Mediation Marketing Toolkit" that includes a marketing video, brochures, audiotapes, and articles about starting and running a practice. Contact the ACR at 1527 New Hampshire Ave., N.W., Washington, DC 20036; (202) 667–9700 or check their Web site: www.acresolution.org.

SPECIALTY MEDIATORS

An increasing number of private practice mediators these days are choosing to specialize in areas other than divorce. The advantages of specializing include the opportunity to become expert in one area, which not only can improve the quality of your work but simplify your life because you don't have to keep up with developments in so many different fields. Another advantage is that, by specializing, you can narrow the focus of your marketing and better target referral sources. For example, people who specialize in construction mediation—one of the more lucrative areas in which to specialize—can focus their marketing efforts on a clearly defined group of potential clients: attorneys who handle construction litigation; developers, architects, and engineers; claims adjusters at commercial insurers; and major contractors. That's still a lot of people to cultivate as clients, but it's at least focused and manageable.

Another area of specialty that has emerged in recent years is employment disputes. Federal and state laws aimed at protecting employees from discrimination based on age, sex, religion, and disability have made employees much more likely to file claims for discrimination and wrongful termination. At the same time, employers have become more willing to use mediation to avoid potentially expensive lawsuits. For mediators specializing in this area, the potential referral sources are well defined and include human resource officers, middle managers at major corporations, and lawyers who themselves specialize in employment cases.

If you're thinking of developing a specialty practice, consider whether you are already in a field that would allow you to become a mediator with that same specialty, thus starting out with an expertise in the subject matter. For example, if you are a civil engineer, construction mediation might be the natural area in which to specialize. If you are a teacher, education and school-based mediation would be a natural specialty, and so on.

When he practiced law many years ago, Christopher Kauders learned enough about personal injury cases so that when he decided to change careers and become a mediator, it was an area in which he could specialize. "As a lawyer, I did just enough personal injury work so I could talk the talk," he recalls, "but I was never known in the field as either a plaintiff or defense lawyer, so as a mediator I'm acceptable to both sides" (personal communication, March 2001).

Since 1987, Kauders has been a full-time mediator, practicing in Boston under the name Pre-Trial Solutions, Inc. He mediates about three hundred cases a year, about half involving personal injury claims. He advises:

> To make a living as a mediator, the good thing about PI [personal injury] as a specialty is that it is a big percentage of any court's docket, and you see the same attorneys and adjusters over and over again. Many claims I mediate have not yet been filed as lawsuits, however, so you've got to market to the claims adjusters as well as to the lawyers. The disadvantage of PI is that you can settle even the biggest case in a couple of hours or at most a day, so you need a large volume of cases.

Kauders mediates at least twenty cases a month, about 90 percent of which he settles. For a typical two-party case, he charges each party $425 for the first three hours, and if it goes longer, $250 an hour is split between the parties. He estimates that someone running a specialty practice such as his can earn between $75,000 and $150,000 a year if they keep busy.

There are three parts to any mediation practice, advises Kauders: (1) mediating, (2) case administration, and (3) marketing, and you have to be good at all three to survive. "You also need to distinguish yourself from the competition, by being a retired judge or something, or by having a shtick," he says. "People say my shtick is bagels and my seeing-eye dog. I bring bagels to every mediation, and I also bring my seeing eye dog. I'm partially sighted."

Could a mediator who was not previously a lawyer develop a practice like his?

> Someone who's not a lawyer could never make a living doing this work. I'm in favor of nonattorney mediators, but they will not be accepted in the personal injury area of this field. For one thing, the lawyers want you to be able to turn to the injured person at the mediation and say, "In my experience, you're being unrealistic about your demands." Without the cache of being an attorney, you're just not going to be able to do that and so you're not going to get the business. I know many fabulous nonattorney mediators who just cannot get this kind of work. [personal communication, March 2001]

For the rest of his practice, Kauders arbitrates commercial disputes and mediates employment cases, including sex- and age-discrimination claims and, more recently, "dot-com lay-offs." He doesn't handle divorce cases, although he recognizes they offer a certain advantage over a specialty in PI. "Unlike PI cases, divorces never settle in one session. They become a cash cow for many sessions. In comparison, PI is a series of one-night stands."

Kauders says he doesn't worry much about competition from other full-time mediators. "The barriers to entry are conference space and staff." Kauders himself employs two assistants who do scheduling and paperwork, and he says that's costly. He estimates that it costs him more than $100 in staff time just to schedule a case.

Despite the demands of running a specialty mediation practice, Kauders is happy with his choice of career. "I love it," he says. "I love helping the parties solve the disputes. It's tiring. It can be grueling. But I love it."

For more information on Christopher Kauders, contact Pre-Trial Solutions, Inc., at (617) 720–2001, or visit his Web site: www.pre-trialsolutions.com.

Some mediators' areas of specialty change over time. In Los Angeles, for example, Jeffrey Krivis, a lawyer by training, mediates through a company he founded in 1990 called First Mediation Corp. "My personal specialties have evolved over the years," he explains. "I started off in personal injury and have now transitioned to employment. Of course I do lots of other cases, ranging from intellectual property to construction, but most people who use me know me in the employment and insurance area."

Krivis estimates he has personally mediated more than three thousand cases. As to how much one can make as a specialty mediator, he says it depends, in part, on where you live. "My sense is that California pays better than most states," he says, and he attributes this condition to the influence of several high-priced mediators. "They started charging a ton of money years ago and set the tone for the rest of the state."

Krivis continues:

> A good, solid personal injury mediator can bill $300,000 to $600,000 per year. After paying a private ADR company for administrative services, the mediator keeps about 50 to 60 percent of the gross. Independent mediators like myself keep about 80 percent of the gross. My billings last year were over $1,000,000. I'm probably on

the high end in the field, though there are several retired judges who bill more.

To learn more about Jeffrey Krivis's practice, contact First Mediation Corporation through its Web site: www.firstmediation.com.

GENERAL MEDIATORS

Among the most satisfying types of mediation practice, but perhaps the toughest to establish, may be a general practice—one in which you handle a variety of cases. In the early days of mediation—in the 1980s and 1990s—it would have been nearly impossible for even the most skilled mediator to make a living as a general practitioner. Outside of a few specialty areas like insurance or construction, awareness of mediation wasn't widespread enough for people to refer enough cases to a general mediator. Fortunately, that has changed for the better, and today it is possible, though still difficult, to make a living as a general mediator. In fact, some very able, energetic, and ambitious people are doing it.

One's general practice will vary, of course, according to what the local market offers as well as one's background, interest, and skills. Successful independent practitioners, however, do have a few things in common. First, they practice in large communities where the market is large enough to sustain their business. Second, they are good at promoting themselves and their practices by writing articles, speaking, teaching, tending their Web sites, and so on. Third, they are very, very busy; if they're not mediating cases, they are soliciting new ones. But they love it. That's why they do it and why they succeed.

Moshe Cohen conducts his general mediation practice, which he calls The Negotiating Table, in Cambridge, Massachusetts. Cohen, who holds a bachelor's degree in physics and a master's degree in engineering, as well as an M.B.A., worked twelve years in engineering and project management before making a career change in 1995 and becoming a mediator.

"As someone with a general mediation practice," he says, "I have to build a house out of a whole lot of little bricks. I do a little of this and a little of that. To be successful in this way, you have to have a long-term view and keep at it. I've been at it for six years, and I'm still in the building phase."

In the past five years, Cohen estimates he's done between two and three hundred mediations. Early on, while he continued his work as an engineer, Cohen did almost all his cases pro bono, that is, without a fee. Many of these cases (he estimates more than 150) were referred to him through a court-connected program. "I did those pro bono cases," he explains, "because coming into this field without being an attorney and without having the natural marketing outlet that being an attorney would have given me, my entree to the field was experience, and the quickest way to get experience was through pro bono."

Once he gained experience, however, he still needed paying clients. "As a nonlawyer in this field," he says, "you face tremendous challenges. People don't go to mediation on their own; they go to their attorney who then has a strong bias in favor of attorneys when they select a mediator."

To overcome this hurdle, Cohen focused on the business community. "All these other attorney-mediators are connected to the legal community in ways I'm never going to be, but a lot of business people don't like lawyers and are glad to use a businessperson as a mediator if they know one." To develop his contacts with people in business, Cohen writes a regular column on negotiation and conflict management for a weekly Boston business newspaper, gives presentations to area business groups, and spends a great deal of time meeting with potential clients. "There was a period for about a year," he recalls, "when I never had breakfast at home. I was always going to some sort of Chamber of Commerce breakfast or other networking group to meet people and make connections."

Today, about half of Cohen's cases involve some kind of business dispute. These include contract cases, partnership dissolutions, and employment disputes between companies and employees. He also mediates securities cases through the panel of the National Association of Securities Dealers, employment cases through the U.S. Postal Service, and employment discrimination cases through the EEOC.

Cohen does some divorce mediation, but not much. "I don't particularly like doing divorce mediation, and it's hard to keep up with it without doing it full-time, so often I bring in a co-mediator to help me. But then I end up making less money at it."

Cohen's standard fee for mediating is $150 an hour, but he plans to raise that soon, for at least some of his cases, to $200 an hour. "Most cases resolve after three hours or so," he explains, "and you've put other time into it setting the case up, doing paperwork and such, so on average you can make maybe $500 a day."

Cohen also does corporate training, which he describes as "a lucrative part of the practice." He regularly presents workshops to businesses on negotiation and mediation and teaches a course on negotiation in the M.B.A. program at Boston University.

In terms of revenue, his mediation practice has grown 50 percent annually for each of the last two years, says Cohen. "And indications are, I'm on track to do it again this year. But I'm still relatively early into this. When I started, I was told it takes five to ten years to establish a mediation practice. I'm just six years into it, and I'm still getting established."

For more information about The Negotiating Table, contact Moshe Cohen at (617) 577–0101, or visit his Web site: www.negotiatingtable.com.

Some independent mediators, particularly those aiming to develop a general practice, find it advantageous to affiliate with another firm that can refer them extra cases. One example is Mosten Mediation Centers, Inc., a private company based in Sherman Oaks, California, that is developing a national network of mediation service providers. Mediators in private practice who affiliate with Mosten continue to run their own practices but are eligible to receive case referrals from the national office.

"If you're a local mediator in private practice," explains Mosten vice president James McPherson, "there are people who live two blocks from you who don't know you're a mediator. One day, they find their partnership agreement has an ADR clause and the other side wants to mediate, so they go on the Web and find Mosten Mediation. They find us before they find you, and we turn around and send you the case."

Mosten's relations with mediators are nonexclusive. Explains McPherson, "We encourage our mediators to market their own practices. We're only providing supplemental cases." When a case is referred, the mediator sets his or her fee within a range of $90 and $250 an hour and splits the proceeds 50–50 with Mosten.

Currently, Mosten has affiliations with about 125 mediators working out of fifty centers in twenty-five states (nineteen in California). Affiliates must have fifty hours of mediation training, one hundred hours of paid mediation experience, and be in good standing in the profession. "Ultimately," says McPherson, "we're going to be in every major center in the country providing cost-effective, mediated solutions."

For more information on Mosten Mediation Centers, contact the company at (800) 286-0777 or check their Web site: www.mostenmediation.com.

A NOTE ON PART-TIME WORK

The stories just recounted are largely about mediators who have set up their own practices and become so successful they have been able to mediate full-time. As several note, however, establishing a private practice is a tough row to hoe, and it's not always possible or advisable to give up one's day job while doing it.

It's worth remembering, too, that many independent mediators never do get to the point of mediating full-time. Instead, they keep their day jobs, whatever they are, and enjoy their mediation practice alongside. By one observer's estimate, of two thousand mediators at a recent convention, probably no more than 10 percent truly mediate full-time. So if a part-time mediation practice is all you want or are able to develop, you'll be in good company and don't need to feel outside the professional mainstream.

In Chapter Three, we discussed the several categories of mediation services. The final category included corporate in-house mediation programs, professional associations, and mediation services run to serve distinct population groups. As these services generally don't employ significant numbers of mediators, I have not addressed them in this chapter. However, these types of service may offer employment opportunities in mediation support—our topic in the next chapter.

7

Job Opportunities in Mediation Support

"Most people, after doing their first mediation, levitate for a time," notes Mark Appel, senior vice president of the American Arbitration Association (AAA). "Your hat size grows three-fold; you feel wonderful and want to do nothing but mediate for the rest of your career."

"But the sad fact is," he continues, speaking for himself and not the AAA, "there isn't a big enough market yet for so many mediators. There aren't jobs out there for everyone."

Appel's observation—which I first mentioned in the Introduction and restate here for emphasis—is correct. Most of us would love to spend all our time mediating—and some get to do just that—but the market isn't quite there yet. The good news, however, is that plenty of jobs *support* the practice of mediation, so everyone interested in the field can find a position.

My own experience bears this out. I've worked, over the years, not only as a mediator but as a program director at a community mediation center, as a sales representative and case manager at private mediation firms, and as a trainer. All these positions and many more like them are essential to the mediation field and many actually pay better than mediating.

So if you don't have the opportunity to find a paid position as a mediator or if you like mediation but your personality and skills better suit you to a nonmediating role, this chapter will help you identify some of the opportunities available in mediation support. We'll consider job opportunities in management and sales (including administration, case management, and sales and development), as well as in education (training and teaching).

Unlike some of the mediator jobs we looked at in the previous chapter in which lawyers sometimes have an advantage, the jobs in mediation support truly are open to all. In fact, for many of them it's an advantage to have a background in something other than law, such as management, sales, or teaching.

Table 7.1 summarizes specific jobs in mediation support, typical education and work backgrounds, and how much you might be able to make in each type of position. This chart and the one presented at the beginning of Chapter Six together present most of the present job opportunities in the field of mediation.

If you are searching for a position in mediation support, at the time of this writing the following are among the sites that carry such listings, and the source for most of the job notices excerpted in this chapter:

> www.mediate.com (follow prompts to The Alternative Newsletter: A Resource Newsletter on Dispute Resolution) www.acresolution.org (the Association for Conflict Resolution)
>
> www.nafcm.org (National Association for Community Mediation)
>
> www.fresno.edu/pacs/rjjobs (Restorative Justice Job Openings at the Center for Peacemaking and Conflict Studies, Fresno Pacific University).

Unless a mediator works entirely alone, he or she is going to be part of an organization that will require some people to run it and others to bring in the business. From the most humble community mediation center to the largest private ADR company, all mediation services need some people to create and implement programs and manage the office, and others to go out and drum up business.

Table 7.1. Opportunities in Mediation Support

Management		Sales and Development		Education	
Administration	Case Management	Sales	Development	Training	Teaching
Positions					
Executive Director ADR Coordinator	Case Manager	Sales Director Account Representative	Development Director Fundraiser	Training Director Trainer Training Assistant	Professor Associate or Assistant Professor, or Adjunct
Organization					
Community mediation center, government agency, private ADR firm, international organization	Community mediation center, government agency, private ADR firm	Private ADR firms, community mediation centers	Community mediation centers, nonprofit ADR research-advocacy groups	Community center, private firm, or independent	College or university; degree or certificate program

(Continued)

Table 7.1. Continued

	Management		Sales and Development		Education	
	Administration	Case Management	Sales	Development	Training	Teaching
Experience and Qualifications	Management, budgeting, mediation; for government, degree in public administration	Service- and detail-oriented; strong communication and people skills	Sales, business, good people skills; may need to travel	Fundraising, grant writing, public relations	Highest earners work full-time and supplement with training; others work part-time	Master's in conflict resolution, social work, law, political science; Ph.D. in conflict resolution
Full- or Part-Time	Executive director positions typically full-time	Typically full-time; could job-share at nonprofit center	Full-time with private firms; often part-time with nonprofits	Part-time with most community centers; full-time with larger nonprofits	Often part-time with mediation practice; full-time possible with community center or private firm	Part-time as adjunct or assistant; tenure-track full-time

Management		Sales and Development		Education	
Administration	Case Management	Sales	Development	Training	Teaching
Compensation					
$30K to $60K with community centers; $75K to $95K with government agency; $100K+ with private firm	20K at nonprofits; up to $50K with private ADR firm	With private ADR, salary or commission $50K to $100K; $25K with nonprofits	$20K to $25K with community centers; up to $50 or $60K with large nonprofits	$50+ per hour as independent; $20K+ with nonprofit center; $50K with private firm	Regular academic salaries supplemented with consulting or mediating

Next we'll consider job opportunities in administration and case management, and in sales and development.

ADMINISTRATION

Running a mediation service can be particularly challenging. You're dealing with clients, all of whom are involved in conflict and usually anxious about the process and the outcome; you're coordinating the schedules of dozens of mediators, all of whom have differing skill levels, backgrounds, areas of expertise, and expectations for income; and you must provide physical space for secure and quiet sessions, all the while adhering to the rules of mediation and the laws of confidentiality. If you're in the private sector, you have to invoice quickly and accurately not just one client but always two and sometimes half a dozen, depending on the number of parties in a case.

Administering a mediation service is challenging, but if you do it well, you'll have the satisfaction of knowing you made it possible not only for people to resolve hundreds of disputes a year but for the mediators themselves to do their work in a safe, efficient, and pleasant environment. All in all, you'll have helped in a tangible way to create a more peaceful and civil community.

COMMUNITY MEDIATION

Let's first consider job possibilities at community mediation centers. Just as these nonprofit centers are an excellent place to start out as a mediator, they also offer good entry-level positions in administration. As we've noted, there are hundreds of centers nationwide; in many states, each county or district has its own center. Each facility requires its own administrator, usually called the executive director. Typically, the executive director manages the center's fiscal operations, including budgeting and grants administration. The executive director also manages the staff, oversees volunteer mediators and interns, and, if time and skills permit, may mediate some of the more challenging cases that are referred to the center. Depending on the size of the staff, there may be an assistant or two as well.

Here's a help-wanted ad for an executive director, excerpted from an ad posted on the Web by a center in the Midwest. It's typical both in terms of job description, required background, and salary.

EXECUTIVE DIRECTOR

Creative and organized individual sought for community mediation program with a staff of seven. Candidates must have significant mediation experience, a minimum of two years experience in administration, grant writing, budgeting, and public relations, and a commitment to working in a collaborative team environment.

Salary: $30,000–$32,000, full-time with exceptional benefits, including health insurance, dental, life, disability, retirement, sick bank, and flexible benefits plan.

As you can see, salaries for community mediation center executive directors are modest. "It's definitely not a six-figure career path; it's barely a five-figure career path," acknowledges Craig Coletta, coordinator for the National Association for Community Mediation, which represents about half the centers nationwide.

Centers in big cities would pay considerably more than the $30,000 advertised—maybe up to twice that amount—but still, these are nonprofits and the pay is going to be modest. The low pay for these jobs tends to create a high turnover, as people work for the nonprofits a few years and then move to higher-paying positions in government or the private sector. This creates, in Coletta's opinion, "a brain drain at community mediation centers"—a problem his organization and others are working to halt by seeking funding to increase pay scales for community mediation center staff.

The good news, however, is that the high turnover makes these administrative positions available on a regular basis. Scanning the various mediation-job Web sites one day, I easily found at least a half-dozen executive director positions available.

To find openings for administrative positions in community mediation, visit the National Association for Community Mediation Web site (www.nafcm.org) and follow the links to "jobs."

Government. Salaries for government administrators are more competitive. We examined many government programs in Chapter Six, among them the mediation program run by the EEOC. As an example of the background, duties, and salary of an administrator of a government mediation program, consider the following profile of Loretta Feller, ADR coordinator for the EEOC's Cleveland district office.

ADMINISTRATOR PROFILE

Name: Loretta Feller

Title: ADR coordinator

Mediation Service: EEOC District Office, Cleveland, Ohio; also serves as volunteer president of Mediation Association of Northeast Ohio

Educational Background: Master's in public administration with a specialty in human resources; bilingual in English and Spanish

Years in this Position: 6

Previous Position: Supervisor, EEOC investigations

Duties: Supervises three staff mediators and support staff; recruits and supervises forty-five external mediators; mediates about twenty cases herself a year out of annual office caseload of about four hundred cases.

Salary: $73,900–$96,100

Satisfactions of the Job: "People say, 'Don't make a federal case out of it,' but when they come to EEOC, they've already made it a federal case. I get a lot of satisfaction seeing them resolve these matters by crafting a solution that meets their needs. When I started, I was kind of taken aback by the expressions of gratitude I received. The parties would come up and pump my hand and say 'Thank you, thank you.' Better yet, occasionally they actually reconcile, and come to understand each other better."

Many state governments also run mediation programs, and they too offer opportunities for administrative employment. For example, the Ohio Commission on Dispute Resolution and Conflict Management is a state agency with a staff of seven that provides information on dispute resolution and training to schools, communities, courts, and other government agencies in Ohio. Recently, the commission ran an ad, from which the following is excerpted, for an administrative position.

DIRECTOR OF COMMUNITY PROGRAMS

Ohio Commission on Dispute Resolution and Conflict Management

Responsible for dispute resolution programming and service delivery; works to initiate and sustain community conflict resolution programs and services, building partnerships among community organizations, schools, courts, and state and local government.

Full-time Salary Range: $35,000–$41,000

Similar administrative positions are available with local mediation programs, colleges and universities, and international organizations. As examples, here are a few recently posted job openings:

- Executive Director (supervises senior staff and manages $800,000 budget toward implementing conflict resolution program in area schools), "Peace Games," Boston, Massachusetts

- Coordinator of Certificate Program in Conflict Resolution (program administration and development; ten-month part-time position averaging seventeen hours per week), Bryn Mawr College Graduate School of Social Work, Bryn Mawr, Pennsylvania

- Associate Director of Conflict Resolution Program (monitoring fifteen to twenty international conflicts, including civil wars; requires master's degree and five years of related international experience); Carter Center, Atlanta, Georgia

- Coordinator for Peace-Building and Demilitarization Program (requires commitment to Quaker values), American Friends Service Committee

- Community Director for Burundi (promotes national reconciliation through communication), Search for Common Ground

For current information on job openings for administrators, check the various Web sites listed at the beginning of this chapter.

CASE MANAGEMENT

If I didn't have the opportunity to be a mediator but believed in the dispute resolution process and enjoyed working with people, I think the job I would most like would be that of case manager.

Every mediation service—nonprofit, governmental, for-profit—is, to a large extent, dependent for its success on the skill of its case managers—the people who have the first contact with prospective disputants and gently and skillfully shepherd them to the mediation table.

What the case manager does is take information from the party who first contacts the center, explains what mediation is, how it works, what it costs, and so on. Then, typically, the case manager contacts the other party to try to get an agreement to mediate. Often the second party is ignorant of mediation and suspicious of any service the first party contacted. The skilled case manager, however, can educate and reassure that party to the point where an initial "no" to mediation becomes a "yes." I've seen it happen many, many times, and often the reluctant party ends up thanking the case manager for persisting in getting both sides to the table.

Case managers are also responsible for helping the parties select a mediator, scheduling the session, generating needed paperwork, obtaining fee deposits on time, and generally making sure the process runs smoothly and professionally.

A typical ad for a case manager by a nonprofit mediation service is this one from a center in the Midwest. No salary range was specified, but something in the area of $25,000 would be expected.

CASE MANAGER

Center for Conflict Resolution
Chicago, Illinois

Exciting opportunity to break into the mediation field. CCR, a nonprofit provider of conflict management services, seeks a full-time case manager. Responsibilities include client screening, scheduling, maintaining case records, supervising volunteer mediator performance, and mediating.

Qualified candidate must be bilingual in Spanish and English, have ready access to a car, possess excellent organization and communication skills, be able to work in a team environment, have seasoned computer skills.

Sometimes you might find a case manager position called by a different name, such as *administrative assistant*. In other instances, as when a dispute resolution service tends to do more arbitration than mediation and therefore must adhere more closely to legal procedures—a job that is essentially one of case management may be referred to as *legal assistant*, as in the following ad from the National Association of Securities Dealers (NASD).

LEGAL ASSISTANT

National Association of Securities Dealers

Analyze submitted papers on assigned cases to ensure jurisdiction and fee meet NASD requirements. Send out hearing notices, handle prehearing motions and correspondence, prepare file for hearing, respond to telephone inquiries from parties, consolidate arbitrator lists.

Requirements: bachelor's degree or equivalent, a paralegal certificate, experience as legal assistant, familiarity with legal terminology. Good written and interpersonal communication and competent on a desk top computer.

The very best private ADR companies have learned the importance of good case management. For example, the largest national firm, JAMS, employs between fifty and seventy case managers, about one for every two or three mediators.

"Case managers are vital to the neutrality and administration of the whole process," says Deana Kardel, JAMS vice president for marketing. "They become the point of contact for the parties, explaining the range of ADR formats available, bringing the parties together to agree on who the neutral will be, and the location, date, and time of the session. They're on the phone a lot and talk to the parties more than the neutrals do," she continues. "Many clients come to know and trust the case managers as much as the neutrals" (personal communication, April 2001).

Kardel says JAMS case managers earn in the $30,000 to $60,000 range, depending on location, and have various backgrounds. "Some were paralegals, legal secretaries, executive assistants," she says. "They're all service-oriented and detail-oriented and like phone work. They're people who are good with people, and quick studies."

SALES AND DEVELOPMENT

If there are no cases coming into a mediation office, there is nothing for mediators to mediate. Someone has to be out in the community looking for cases. This holds for nonprofit mediation services as well as private ADR companies. If you are skilled in sales or marketing, the mediation field offers plenty of opportunities.

In the private sector, most ADR companies employ several salespeople to call on businesses or agencies that can refer cases for mediation or arbitration. Typically, referral sources include insurance companies, court administrators, law departments in major corporations, and law firms.

When I started my own private ADR company, for example, I spent most of the first year driving among several cities in our region, giving hour-long presentations to groups of adjusters at insurance company claims offices. I'd explain how mediation could help resolve claims for personal injury and property damage, show a video of a typical mediation session, and then explain how to submit cases to our company for what we hoped would be rapid and successful resolution through mediation or arbitration. On the way home, I'd stop at a couple of law firms and try to get a few minutes with the head of the litigation department to make a similar pitch. More than half the insurance companies referred cases to us, often within weeks or a couple of months; responses from law firms were about the same, although the referrals tended to be much slower, often taking many months or even years.

Some ADR companies pay their salespeople a salary; others pay on commission, based on the amount of business generated.

An unusual aspect of sales in the mediation field is that sometimes a firm's sales rep must sell not only the idea of mediation but the actual mediators. As we noted earlier, when parties select a mediation service, particularly for large, complex cases involving significant amounts of money, they often choose a mediation service based on the particular mediators available on that company's roster. Therefore, companies that handle major cases often promote themselves by promoting the individual mediators on their panels.

An example is JAMS. At each of its major offices, JAMS employs a special kind of salesperson it calls a *practice development manager*. This person's job is to increase business by helping the company's mediators present themselves effectively to businesses and law firms that might refer cases to the company. "The practice development managers help the mediators promote themselves," explains Deana Kardel, vice president for marketing. She continues:

> Our mediators are mostly retired judges, and unless they were elected they haven't had much experience putting themselves out in a marketing function. So when mediators join us, we put out a press release, look for marketing and speaking opportunities, then help them with their Power Point presentations and media relations.

Salaries for JAMS practice development managers are about $75,000—and higher in large cities like New York and San Francisco.

Nonprofit mediation centers also rely on marketing people to get the word out in the community about the availability of their services. Their task is to call on judges, court clerks, prosecutors, and community groups like neighborhood associations to encourage them to refer cases. The position, which might be called something like *community relations specialist* would likely pay in the

$20,000 to $25,000 range in a midsize community and maybe half again as much in a large city.

The nonprofit mediation world also must rely on fundraising, an endless process of seeking financial support. At the local level, community mediation centers typically employ a full- or part-time development director whose job it is to call on local funding sources. Typically, these would include local and state government agencies, broad-based charities such as United Way, and private foundations and individuals. Fundraising activities are ongoing, including regular mailings to solicit support and special events such as award dinners.

Development positions at regional or national nonprofits can pay quite well, as shown in the following excerpt from an ad for a combination "development and research director."

DEVELOPMENT AND RESEARCH DIRECTOR

California Dispute Resolution Institute, San Francisco

The Institute is an educational nonprofit that works to promote sound, well-informed policy making by sponsoring conferences and dialogues.

Development and research director handles all research projects, manages the Web site, prepares and presents reports, and maintains contacts with funding agencies and leaders in the dispute resolution community.

Position is half- to full-time.

Salary Range: $50,000–$60,000

Available positions in sales and development can be found on the various mediation Web sites listed at the beginning of this chapter, but if you have a background either in sales or development and want to work in mediation, I'd encourage you to call any local, regional, or national firm in which you're interested. My guess is they will be glad to hear from you and willing to consider what you have to offer.

EDUCATION

I noted in Chapter Five that as more people seek to become mediators, there is an increasing demand for trainers, as well as for teachers and professors of conflict resolution. The demand is evident from elementary, middle, and high schools right up through college and graduate programs. If you love the idea of mediation but your strength is in academics, becoming a trainer or a teacher of conflict resolution may offer you a satisfying career. In an important way, you will also help advance the entire field of mediation: some of the people you train may go on to found new ADR companies, government mediation programs, or nonprofit organizations that promote conflict resolution, thus creating jobs for even more mediators in the future.

TRAINING

Training is a broad category that includes just about any kind of instruction done outside a college or university. Many mediators make training a minor component of their practice; it's a way to pick up some extra income and to meet a lot of people, some of whom might later refer cases to mediate. Other mediators come to find that they enjoy training so much and they are so good at it that training becomes their primary work, and they end up mediating only on the side.

My own experience in training is, I think, typical for someone who is not a full-time trainer. Over the years, for example, I've taught basic mediation skills to

- Civil court judges interested in referring cases to mediation

- Mid-level corporate managers who wanted to learn to resolve disputes among their employees

- Attorneys who wanted to understand mediation in order to recommend it to their clients

- Middle school students who had been selected to act as mediators in a school-sponsored program of peer mediation

- Recently retired judges about to join the panel of a private ADR firm

- Teenage counselors at a summer camp seeking skills to resolve disputes that might arise among themselves or their campers

Nearly all community mediation centers hire part- or full-time trainers to train groups of local people to become volunteer mediators. Often a center also develops programs to train local business and professional groups in basic conflict resolution, as well as local students participating in peer mediation programs.

The job notice excerpted next outlines a typical set of responsibilities for a community mediation center trainer.

TRAINING COORDINATOR

Good Shepherd Mediation Program, Philadelphia

Preparing and presenting conflict resolution, anger management, meeting facilitation, and mediation training, as required by schools, private and public agencies, and neighborhood organizations.

A degree in education, conflict resolution, social work, communications, or a related degree is needed. Seeking experienced mediator with training and interpersonal and communication skills.

Salary: High $20,000s

The relatively low salary offered for the training position is, unfortunately, not unusual for a community mediation center. When private firms hire trainers, however, the salaries can be substantially higher. For example, CDR Associates, a national conflict resolution training organization based in Boulder, Colorado, maintains a staff of highly qualified trainers. A trainer working at the national level with an organization such as CDR could make a salary in the range of $50,000 per year.

If you prefer to work on your own rather than with an organization, you can set up on your own as an independent trainer. One independent trainer I know developed a nice part-time practice locally just doing peer mediation training in the local schools, charging $50 to $75 an hour for a twelve-hour program. Trainers who specialize in divorce mediation and become approved by the ACR generally charge upwards of $1,000 for a basic forty-hour training course. Other trainers specialize in industrial relations, delivering the message of conflict resolution primarily to corporate managers as a way to improve their skills in handling workplace conflicts. These trainers generally can earn about $2,000 for a full-day or perhaps a two-day training course for mid-level managers.

Obviously, before you can launch a career as a mediation trainer, you'll need to get trained yourself and get some solid experience mediating. You'd then want to take advanced training to further develop your skills; the more training you take, the better trainer you're likely to become. In addition, the people you learn from will become good contacts in the field and help you develop your own career as a trainer.

TEACHING

As we discussed in Chapter Five, dozens of colleges and universities today offer master's and doctoral programs in conflict resolution. Many others offer individual courses and certificate programs. This creates a new, strong demand for those capable of teaching these courses. For example, the recent job notice excerpted next concerns an opening for one such position in a political science department.

ASSISTANT PROFESSOR IN CONFLICT MANAGEMENT

Kent State University, Ohio

The Department of Political Science invites applications for a non-tenure-track, full-time appointment. Competitive salary and incentives as well as collaborative and individual research initiatives offered. Ph.D. in conflict resolution or closely related field is required.

Courses to be taught include Introduction to Conflict Management, Conflict Theory, Cross-Cultural Conflict Management, Negotiation, and Nonviolence: Theory and Practice.

If your strength is in teaching, there has never been a better time to pursue an academic career in conflict resolution. Many academicians combine their teaching with actual mediation, sometimes finding a niche for themselves on the panels of private ADR companies or (this is more likely) helping set up and oversee mediation systems to resolve disputes within the university community. Others consult with officials in government and industry, advising on how to apply theories of conflict resolution to actual public policy disputes.

For information on colleges and universities that may offer teaching positions in conflict resolution, see the discussion of degree programs in Chapter Five. For a comprehensive list produced by Nova University of more than seventy-five college and university programs (including those offering certificates) see the Web site: www.nova.edu/shss/DCAR.

SERVICE

I hope the opportunities in mediation support I've discussed (in management, sales and development, and education), together with actual jobs in mediating discussed in Chapter Six, provide helpful guidance toward a career path for you into the field of mediation.

However, even if circumstances do not allow you to pursue a career in mediation or mediation support, you can still participate in this field in a meaningful way by contributing your time or money. Each of the hundreds of community mediation centers have boards of directors who oversee their operations and help guide their growth. Serving as a board member of the center where you live would be a wonderful way to make a positive contribution to the peaceful future of your community. And if you are able to do so, you can contribute financially to your local community mediation center, or to national research efforts aimed at improving the delivery of mediation services, or to a college that wishes to establish a program in conflict resolution, or to a local middle school that would set up a peer mediation program if only it had the funds to hire a trainer and staff member to run it.

All in all, it is a good time to pursue a career in mediation support. The positions are available, and there is much work to be done.

Afterword

You are not required to complete the work, but nei-
ther are you free to refrain from beginning it.
Chapter 2, "Ethics of the Fathers," The Talmud

If, after reading this book, you do at some point take basic mediator training, I ask that you do just one thing. Even if, for whatever
reason, you do not pursue a career in mediation—even if you never
mediate a single case—please take your mediation skills home and
use them with the people you love. Use them to help create what
the Bible calls *shalom bayit*—peace in the house. If you do, your
compensation will surpass any salary, commission, or fee you ever
could hope to have earned in the marketplace. And more impor-
tantly, your spouse, your children, whomever you live with, will call
you blessed.

Resources

A. Sample Rules of Mediation

B. Standards of Conduct for Mediators

C. Statewide Mediation Offices

D. National and Regional Mediation Organizations and Services

E. Sample Memoranda of Understanding

Resource A
Sample Rules of Mediation

This set of mediation rules is used by Empire Mediation & Arbitration, Inc., a private dispute resolution company in Rochester, New York. These rules are typical of those used at most mediation services that handle a general variety of cases.

1. MEDIATION DEFINED/ROLE OF THE MEDIATOR: Mediation is a voluntary process in which the parties to the dispute meet together confidentially with a neutral third party called a "mediator." The mediator does not take sides and has no authority to make a decision, but works with the parties to help them evaluate their goals and options in order to find a solution to the dispute satisfactory to all sides.

2. INITIATING THE PROCESS: Any party to a dispute may begin mediation by sending to Empire Mediation & Arbitration, Inc. ("Empire") a completed Submission Form.

3. AGREEMENT TO MEDIATE: Empire will contact all parties to a dispute to determine their willingness to participate in mediation. If the parties agree to participate, each will sign an "Agreement to Mediate" before the commencement of the first mediation session.

4. APPOINTMENT OF MEDIATOR: From its panel of mediators, Empire will propose to the parties the names of one or more mediators qualified and available to mediate their case. The panelist will be chosen by agreement of all the parties.

5. SCHEDULING/NOTICE OF MEDIATION: Empire will schedule the mediation at a time and place convenient to all parties, and notify the parties in writing of the date, time and location of the session. The mediation may be rescheduled upon a party's request but a rescheduling fee will be assessed against the requesting party.

6. REPRESENTATION AT SESSION: Each party must be represented at the mediation by a person with authority to settle the dispute. Individuals may be represented by legal counsel, and counsel are encouraged to have their clients participate. Insurance companies may be represented by claims staff or defense counsel. Other business corporations may be represented by executive staff or counsel. It is not necessary for witnesses to attend the mediation, but if they do, their testimony will be heard at the mediator's discretion.

7. RULES OF EVIDENCE: The rules of evidence common to judicial and arbitral proceedings do not apply in mediation. Any statement, document, or other record offered by the parties will be admissible unless the mediator, in his or her sole discretion, finds it to be irrelevant or otherwise inappropriate in the session.

8. SESSION PROCEDURE-OPENING STATEMENTS: The mediator will commence the session with an Opening Statement in which he or she will explain the purposes and procedures of the session. The parties will then make their opening statements, explaining their positions on the issues in dispute, including the presentation of any documents, photographs, and oral or written summaries of witness testimony that would be helpful to the mediator in understanding the case.

9. SESSION PROCEDURE-PRIVATE CAUCUSES: During the mediation, the mediator may meet in private caucus with each of the parties and counsel, to explore positions and settlement options.

Any information disclosed to the mediator in the caucus will be kept confidential unless the party expressly tells the mediator it may be disclosed to the other parties.

10. CONFIDENTIALITY: The mediation session constitutes a settlement negotiation and statements made during the mediation by the parties are inadmissible, to the extent allowed by law, in subsequent judicial or arbitral proceedings relating to the dispute. The parties will maintain the confidentiality of the mediation and not introduce as evidence in any future arbitral or judicial proceeding statements made by the mediator or by any other party or subpoena a mediator to testify or produce records in any such proceeding. Evidence otherwise discoverable or admissible is not made inadmissible or non-discoverable because of its use in mediation.

11. NO RECORD: No stenographic or other record of the mediation will be made.

12. CONCLUSION OF THE MEDIATION: The mediation will conclude when the parties have reached a settlement agreement, or upon the oral or written request of the parties, or at the discretion of the mediator.

13. SETTLEMENT DOCUMENTS: If a settlement agreement is reached during the mediation, the parties will make their own arrangements for the drafting and later execution of settlement documents.

14. EXCLUSION OF LIABILITY: Mediators conducting sessions for Empire act as independent contractors; they are not employees of the company. Neither mediators nor the company act as legal counsel for any of the parties in the dispute. Parties have the right to legal counsel and are encouraged to obtain legal advice in connection with a dispute. Parties not represented by counsel at a mediation may condition a settlement agreement upon review by their attorney. Neither mediators nor the company are necessary parties in judicial proceedings relating to mediation, and neither the mediator nor the company will be liable to any party for an act or omission in connection with a mediation conducted under these rules.

Resource B
Standards of Conduct for Mediators

These standards were developed by three professional groups: the American Arbitration Association, the American Bar Association, and the Society of Professionals in Dispute Resolution (now merged into the Association for Conflict Resolution). The Standards are intended to apply to all types of mediation, but in some cases their application may be affected by laws or contractual agreements.

I. Self-Determination: A Mediator Shall Recognize that Mediation Is Based on the Principle of Self-Determination by the Parties.

Self-determination is the fundamental principle of mediation. It requires that the mediation process rely upon the ability of the parties to reach a voluntary, uncoerced agreement. Any party may withdraw from mediation at any time.

COMMENTS: The mediator may provide information about the process, raise issues, and help parties explore options. The primary role of the mediator is to facilitate a voluntary resolution of a dispute. Parties shall be given the opportunity to consider all proposed options.

A mediator cannot personally ensure that each party has made a fully informed choice to reach a particular agreement, but it is a

---

Note: Reprinted by permission of the Association for Conflict Resolution.

good practice for the mediator to make the parties aware of the importance of consulting other professionals, where appropriate, to help them make informed decisions.

II. Impartiality: A Mediator Shall Conduct the Mediation in an Impartial Manner.

The concept of mediator impartiality is central to the mediation process. A mediator shall mediate only those matters in which she or he can remain impartial and evenhanded. If at any time the mediator is unable to conduct the process in an impartial manner, the mediator is obligated to withdraw.

COMMENTS: A mediator shall avoid conduct that gives the appearance of partiality toward one of the parties. The quality of the mediation process is enhanced when the parties have confidence in the impartiality of the mediator.

When mediators are appointed by a court or institution, the appointing agency shall make reasonable efforts to ensure that mediators serve impartially.

A mediator should guard against partiality or prejudice based on the parties' personal characteristics, background or performance at the mediation.

III. Conflicts of Interest: A Mediator Shall Disclose All Actual and Potential Conflicts of Interest Reasonably Known to the Mediator. After Disclosure, the Mediator Shall Decline to Mediate Unless All Parties Choose to Retain the Mediator. The Need to Protect Against Conflicts of Interest Also Governs Conduct that Occurs During and After the Mediation.

A conflict of interest is a dealing or relationship that might create an impression of possible bias. The basic approach to questions of conflict of interest is consistent with the concept of self-determination. The mediator has a responsibility to disclose all actual and potential conflicts that are reasonably known to the mediator and could reasonably be seen as raising a question about impartiality. If all parties agree to mediate after being informed of conflicts, the mediator may proceed with the mediation. If, however, the conflict of interest casts serious doubt on the integrity of the process, the mediator shall decline to proceed.

A mediator must avoid the appearance of conflict of interest both during and after the mediation. Without the consent of all parties, a mediator shall not subsequently establish a professional relationship with one of the parties in a related matter, or in an unrelated matter under circumstances which would raise legitimate questions about the integrity of the mediation process.

COMMENTS: A mediator shall avoid conflicts of interest in recommending the services of other professionals. A mediator may make reference to professional referral services or associations which maintain rosters of qualified professionals.

Potential conflicts of interest may arise between administrators of mediation programs and mediators and there may be strong pressures on the mediator to settle a particular case or cases. The mediator's commitment must be to the parties and the process. Pressures from outside of the mediation process should never influence the mediator to coerce parties to settle.

IV. Competence: A Mediator Shall Mediate Only When the Mediator Has the Necessary Qualifications to Satisfy the Reasonable Expectations of the Parties.

Any person may be selected as a mediator, provided that the parties are satisfied with the mediator's qualifications. Training and experience in mediation, however, are often necessary for effective mediation. A person who offers herself or himself as available to serve as a mediator gives parties and the public the expectation that she or he has the competency to mediate effectively. In court-connected or other forms of mandated mediation, it is essential that mediators assigned to the parties have the requisite training and experience.

COMMENTS: Mediators should have available for the parties information regarding their relevant training, education and experience.

The requirements for appearing on a list of mediators must be made public and available to interested persons.

When mediators are appointed by a court or institution, the appointing agency shall make reasonable efforts to ensure that each mediator is qualified for the particular mediation.

V. Confidentiality: A Mediator Shall Maintain the Reasonable Expectations of the Parties with Regard to Confidentiality.

The reasonable expectations of the parties with regard to confidentiality shall be met by the mediator. The parties' expectations of confidentiality depend on the circumstances of the mediation and any agreements they may make. A mediator shall not disclose any matter that a party expects to be confidential unless given permission by all parties or unless required by law or other public policy.

COMMENTS: The parties may make their own rules with respect to confidentiality, or the accepted practice of an individual mediator or institution may dictate a particular set of expectations. Since the parties' expectations regarding confidentiality are important, the mediator should discuss these expectations with the parties.

If the mediator holds private sessions with a party, the nature of these sessions with regard to confidentiality should be discussed prior to undertaking such sessions.

In order to protect the integrity of the mediation, a mediator should avoid communicating information about how the parties acted in the mediation process, the merits of the case, or settlement offers. The mediator may report, if required, whether parties appeared at a scheduled mediation.

Where the parties have agreed that all or a portion of the information disclosed during a mediation is confidential, the parties' agreement should be respected by the mediator.

Confidentiality should not be construed to limit or prohibit the effective monitoring, research, or evaluation of mediation programs by responsible persons. Under appropriate circumstances, researchers may be permitted to obtain access to statistical data and, with the permission of the parties, to individual case files, observations of live mediations, and interviews with participants.

VI. Quality of the Process: A Mediator Shall Conduct the Mediation Fairly, Diligently, and in a Manner Consistent with the Principle of Self-Determination by the Parties.

A mediator shall work to ensure a quality process and to encourage mutual respect among the parties. A quality process requires a commitment by the mediator to diligence and procedural fairness. There should be adequate opportunity for each party in the mediation to participate in the discussions. The parties decide when and under what conditions they will reach an agreement or terminate a mediation.

COMMENTS: A mediator may agree to mediate only when he or she is prepared to commit the attention essential to an effective mediation.

Mediators should only accept cases when they can satisfy the reasonable expectations of the parties concerning the timing of the process. A mediator should not allow a mediation to be unduly delayed by the parties or their representatives.

The presence or absence of persons at a mediation depends on the agreement of the parties and mediator. The parties and mediator may agree that others may be excluded from particular sessions or from the entire mediation process.

The primary purpose of a mediator is to facilitate the parties' voluntary agreement. This role differs substantially from other professional-client relationships. Mixing the role of a mediator and the role of a professional advising a client is problematic, and mediators must strive to distinguish between the roles. A mediator should therefore refrain from providing professional advice. Where appropriate, a mediator should recommend that parties seek outside professional advice, or consider resolving their dispute through arbitration, counseling, neutral evaluation, or other processes. A mediator who undertakes, at the request of the parties, an additional dispute resolution role in the same matter assumes increased responsibilities and obligations that may be governed by the standards of other professions.

A mediator shall withdraw from a mediation when incapable of serving or when unable to remain impartial.

A mediator shall withdraw from the mediation or postpone a session if the mediation is being used to further illegal conduct, or if a party is unable to participate due to drug, alcohol, or other physical or mental incapacity.

Mediators should not permit their behavior in the mediation process to be guided by a desire for a high settlement rate.

VII. Advertising and Solicitation: A Mediator Shall Be Truthful in Advertising and Solicitation for Mediation.

Advertising or any other communication with the public concerning services offered or regarding the education, training, and expertise of the mediator shall be truthful. Mediators shall refrain from promises and guarantees of results.

COMMENTS: It is imperative that communication with the public educate and instill confidence in the process.

In an advertisement or other communication to the public, a mediator may make reference to meeting state, national, or private organization qualifications only if the entity referred to has a procedure for qualifying mediators and the mediator has been duly granted the requisite status.

VIII. Fees: A Mediator Shall Fully Disclose and Explain the Basis of Compensation, Fees, and Charges to the Parties.

The parties should be provided sufficient information about fees at the outset of a mediation to determine if they wish to retain the services of a mediator. If a mediator charges fees, the fees shall be reasonable considering, among other things, the mediation service, the type and complexity of the matter, the expertise of the mediator, the time required, and the rates customary in the community. The better practice in reaching an understanding about fees is to set down the arrangements in a written agreement.

COMMENTS: A mediator who withdraws from a mediation should return any unearned fee to the parties.

A mediator should not enter into a fee agreement which is contingent upon the result of the mediation or amount of the settlement.

Co-mediators who share a fee should hold to standards of reasonableness in determining the allocation of fees.

A mediator should not accept a fee for referral of a matter to another mediator or to any other person.

IX. Obligations to the Mediation Process.

Mediators have a duty to improve the practice of mediation. COMMENTS: Mediators are regarded as knowledgeable in the process of mediation. They have an obligation to use their knowledge to help educate the public about mediation; to make mediation accessible to those who would like to use it; to correct abuses; and to improve their professional skills and abilities.

Resource C
Statewide Mediation Offices

Many states have special offices to coordinate mediation policies and services within the state. Some offices are sponsored or partly funded by state governments; others are independent nonprofit organizations that assume this role themselves. These offices can provide information on mediators and mediation services located within their states. Some offices will actually help mediate disputes involving public policy issues.

The following list is provided by Policy Consensus Initiative, a national nonprofit program to establish and strengthen the use of collaborative practices in states to bring about more effective governance. For updates of this list, visit PCI's Web site at: www.policyconsensus.org.

Alabama

Alabama Center for Dispute Resolution
415 Dexter Avenue
PO BOX 671
Montgomery, AL 36101
(334) 269–1515, ext. 111
www.alabamaADR.org

Arizona

Arizona Supreme Court ADR Program
1501 W. Washington, Suite 411
Phoenix, AZ 85007
(602) 542–9251

Arkansas

Arkansas ADR Commission
Justice Bldg.
625 Marshall St.
Little Rock, AR 72201
(501) 682–9400, ext. 1332
jennifer.jones-taylor@mail.state.ar.us

California

Common Ground, Law & Public Policy Programs
University of California
Davis Research Park
Davis, CA 95616
(916) 757–8569

California Center for Public Dispute Resolution
1303 J Street, Suite 250
Sacramento, CA 95814
(916) 445–2079

Colorado

Office of Dispute Resolution
Colorado Judicial Department
1301 Pennsylvania Street, Suite 110
Denver, CO 80203–2416
(303) 837–3672

Florida

Florida Conflict Resolution Consortium
Florida State University
2031 East Paul Dirac Drive
Tallahassee, FL 32310
(850) 644–6320
flacrc@mailer.fsu.edu

Florida Dispute Resolution Center
Supreme Court Bldg.
Tallahassee, FL 32399
(850) 921–2910
www.flcourts.org/osca/divisions/adr

Georgia

Georgia Office of Dispute Resolution
800 The Hurt Building
50 Hurt Plaza
Atlanta, GA 30303
(404) 527–8789
www.ganet.org/gadr

Hawaii

Center for Alternative Dispute Resolution
The State Judiciary of Hawaii
417 South King St., Room 207
Honolulu, HI 96813
(808) 539–4237
www.state.hi.us/jud/cadr.htm

Indiana

Indiana Conflict Resolution Institute
Indiana University

School of Public and Environmental Affairs #322
1315 E. 10th St.
Bloomington, IN 47405
(812) 855–1618
www.spea.indiana.edu/icri

Iowa

Iowa Peace Institute
917 10th Ave.
PO Box 480
Grinnel, IA 50112
(641) 236–4880
www.iapeace.org

Maryland

Mediation and Conflict Resolution Office for the State of Maryland
113 Townsontown Blvd., Suite C
Towson, MD 21286
(410) 321–2398
rachel.wohl@courts.state.md.us

Massachusetts

Office of Dispute Resolution
Commonwealth of Massachusetts
One Ashburton Place, Room 501
Boston, MA 02108
(617) 727–2224, ext. 21174

Minnesota

Division of Alternative Dispute Resolution
304 Centennial Office Building
St. Paul, MN 55155
(612) 296–2633

Montana

Montana Consensus Council
Office of the Governor
State Capital Building
Helena, MT 59620
(406) 444–2075
mmckinney@state.mt.us

Nebraska

Office of Dispute Resolution
1220 State Capitol
PO Box 98910
Lincoln, NE 68509–8910
(402) 471–3148
whind@nsc.state.ne.us

New Hampshire

Program on Consensus and Conflict Resolution
University of New Hampshire
11 Brookway
Thompson Hall, Rm. 211
Durham, NH 03824
(603) 862–3290
jsv@cixunix.unh.edu

New Jersey

Office of Dispute Settlement
25 Market St.
PO Box 850
Trenton, NJ 08625
(609) 292–7686

New York

New York State Dispute Resolution Association, Inc.
182-A Washington Ave.
Albany, NY 12210
(518) 465–2500
www.nysdra.org

North Carolina

Public Dispute Resolution Program
University of North Carolina Institute of Government
Campus Box 3330
Chapel Hill, NC 27599
(919) 962–5190
http://ncinfo.iog.unc.edu/programs/dispute/index.html

North Carolina Dispute Resolution Commission
1100 Navaho Drive, Suite 126
PO Box 2448
Raleigh, NC 27602
(919) 981–5077
www.aoc.state.nc.us/www/drc

North Dakota

The Consensus Council, Inc.
1003 Interstate Avenue, Suite 7
Bismarck, ND 58503–0500
(701) 224–0588

Ohio

Ohio Commission on Dispute Resolution and Conflict Management
77 South High Street, 24th Floor
Columbus, OH 43215–6108
(614) 752–9595
www.state.oh.us/cdr

Oregon

Oregon Dispute Resolution Commission
1201 Court Street NE, Suite 305
Salem, OR 97310
(503) 378–2877
www.odrc.state.or.us

Texas

Center for Public Policy Dispute Resolution
School of Law
Univ. of Texas at Austin
727 East Dean Keeton Street
Austin, TX 78705
(512) 471–3507

Virginia

Virginia Department of Dispute Resolution
Supreme Court of Virginia
Office of the Executive Secretary
100 North Ninth Street
Richmond, VA 23219
(804) 786–6455

Resource D
National and Regional Mediation
Organizations and Services

Organizations listed in this section can be contacted for more information about the mediation field in general, such as career and training opportunities, state and federal legislation, and references to specific mediators or mediation services in your area.

The mediation services listed include private dispute resolution companies as well as nonprofit groups that provide mediation, arbitration, education, and related services.

MEDIATION ORGANIZATIONS

Association for Conflict Resolution
1527 New Hampshire Ave., N.W., 3rd Floor
Washington, DC 20036
(202) 667–9700
www.acresolution.org

The Association (the merged organization of the Academy of Family Mediators, the Conflict Resolution Education Network, and the Society of Professionals in Dispute Resolution), supports the professional development of more than 7,000 mediators, arbitrators, educators, and others involved in conflict resolution. ACR offers an annual conference, quarterly magazine, scholarly journal, and special reports.

American Bar Association
Section on Dispute Resolution
740 15th St., N.W., 9th Floor
Washington, DC 20005
(202) 662–1680
www.abanet.org/dispute

Monitors and provides information on dispute resolution and the courts, and dispute resolution legislation pending and enacted.

Association of Family and Conciliation Courts
6515 Grand Teton Plaza, Suite 210
Madison, WI 53719
(608) 664–3750
www.afccnet.org

Monitors and provides information on court-sponsored divorce and family mediation and arbitration programs.

Conflict Resolution Center International
204 Thirty-seventh Street
Pittsburgh, PA 152201
(412) 687–6210
www.conflictres.org

The non-profit center promotes non-violent conflict resolution by acting as a resource for information on dispute resolution. The center maintains a library on conflict resolution, publishes a directory of conflict resolvers and organizations, and publishes a quarterly periodical, "Conflict Resolution-Notes."

CPR Institute for Dispute Resolution
366 Madison Avenue, 14th Floor
New York, NY 10017

(212) 949–6490
www.cpradr.org

Encourages large businesses and law firms to use mediation and other dispute resolution techniques as a first resort to settle disputes.

Mediation Information and Resource Center
260 East 15th Ave., Suite E
Eugene, OR 97401
(541) 485–3151
www.mediate.com

The Center, part of Mediate.com, is a library of resources for both mediators and disputants. It offers articles, lists of journals and organizations, and acts as a network for mediator referrals.

National Association for Community Mediation
1527 New Hampshire Ave., N.W.
Washington, DC 20036
(202) 667–9700
www.nafcm.org

Supports the growth of non-profit, community mediation centers, and represents nearly 300 centers in 47 states. Can provide contact information for centers nationwide.

National Center for State Courts
300 Newport Avenue
Williamsburg, VA 23185
(757) 253–2000
(800) 877–1233
www.ncsconline.org

Compiles and analyses statistics on court-connected ADR programs around the country.

MEDIATION SERVICES

American Arbitration Association
335 Madison Ave.
New York, NY 10017, 10th Floor
(212) 716–5880
www.adr.org

Non-profit organization provides information and maintains extensive library on all forms of dispute resolution; sponsors training programs and administers mediation and arbitration programs through offices across the country.

Arbitration Forums, Inc.
3350 Buschwood Park Drive, Suite 295
Tampa, FL 33618
(813) 931–4004
(800) 967–8889
www.arbfile.org

Non-profit organization arbitrates and mediates commercial disputes, particularly those involving the insurance industry through offices nationwide.

Asian Pacific American Dispute Resolution Center
1145 Wilshire Blvd., Suite 100
Los Angeles, CA 90017
(213) 250–8190
www.apadrc.apanet.org

Provides mediation and conciliation services in Asian Pacific languages. Handles cases involving ethnic disputes and race relations, and domestic, housing, neighborhood, employment and business conflicts.

CDR Associates
100 Arapahoe Ave., Suite 12
Boulder, CO 80302
(303) 442–7367
(800) MEDIATE
www.mediate.org

Provides extensive training programs in mediation and conflict management, and mediates major disputes involving corporations, governments, and communities nationally.

Center for Dispute Settlement
1666 Connecticut Ave., NW
Washington, DC 20009
(202) 265–9572

Provides general mediation and arbitrations services, and training.

Dispute Resolution, Inc.
179 Allyn Street, Suite 508
Hartford, CT 06103
(860) 724–0861
(800) 726–2393

Private dispute resolution company, founded in 1983, offers mediation and arbitration of commercial, employment, construction, and personal injury disputes.

Empire Mediation & Arbitration, Inc.
280 Sandringham Road
Rochester, NY 14610
(716) 264–9130

Private dispute resolution firm mediates and arbitrates commercial, interpersonal, and family disputes.

Federal Mediation and Conciliation Service
2100 K Street, N.W.
Washington, DC 20427
(202) 606–8100
www.fmcs.gov.

The FMCS mediates disputes within federal government agencies and between agencies and the public, and trains personnel at other agencies to set up their own dispute resolution systems.

JAMS
1920 Main St., Suite 300
Irvine, CA 92614
(949) 224–4600
(800) 352-JAMS
www.jamsadr.com

JAMS—the name used to stand for "Judicial Arbitration & Mediation"—is the largest, national private dispute resolution company. Through offices nationwide, JAMS mediates and arbitrates a wide range of commercial disputes.

Lesbian and Gay Community Services Center
Mediation Services/Project Resolve
208 West 13th St.
New York, NY 10011
(212) 620–7310
www.gaycenter.org

This program helps lesbian, gay, bisexual, transgender, and people with HIV/AIDS and their families to resolve conflicts outside the court system.

Resolute Systems, Inc.
1550 North Prospect Ave.
Milwaukee, WI 53202

(414) 276–4774
(800) 776–6060
www.resolutesystems.com

Private dispute resolution company with five offices nationally; mediates and arbitrates wide range of commercial disputes.

Resolve, Inc.
1255 23rd St., NW, Suite 275
Washington, DC 20037
(202) 944–2300
www.resolv.org

Specializes in resolving environmental disputes.

Solutions with Consensus, Inc.
Abrams Bank Center
PO Box 181496
Dallas, TX 75218
(972) 661–3771
(800) 574–4744
www.solutionswithconsensus.com

Private dispute resolution company provides mediation and arbitration of commercial and domestic disputes, and extensive conflict resolution training.

U.S. Arbitration & Mediation, Inc.
National Administrative Office
800 Roosevelt Road, Suite A-5
Glen Ellyn, IL 60137
(800) 318–2700
www.usam.com

Network of national offices providing general mediation and arbitration of commercial disputes.

Western Network
1350 San Juan Drive
Santa Fe, New Mexico 87505
(505) 982–9805
(800) 326–9805

Specializes in public policy disputes involving natural resources and environmental regulation and which affect relations between communities, organized interest groups and government.

Resource E
Sample Memoranda of Understanding

The final, written work-product of a divorce mediator is often a Memorandum of Understanding, a document expressing, in plain English, the agreements a couple has reached. Following are two sample memoranda provided by mediator Arnold Shienvold. Dr. Shienvold is currently president of the Association for Conflict Resolution. He also served as past president of the former Academy of Family Mediators. Dr. Shienvold maintains a private practice in Harrisburg, Pennsylvania, where he does mediation, facilitation, forensic evaluations, and psychotherapy. Names and other identifying information in these memoranda have been altered to protect the confidentiality of the families involved.

The first memorandum, prepared for "Tom and Mary Doe," a couple with two children, primarily addresses financial issues, such as child and spousal support, and property and asset distribution. The second memorandum, for "Wanda and Lloyd Banks," concerns parenting arrangements for the couple's son.

MEMORANDUM OF UNDERSTANDING

Tom and Mary Doe

Tom and Mary Doe have mutually agreed to terminate their marriage. To that end they have worked together to reach the following agreements regarding the custody of their children, the division of their assets, and the providing of child and spousal support.

I.   Custody

     A.   With respect to the custody of their children, Bobby and Sue, Tom and Mary will share the legal custody. Mary's house, however, shall be designated as the primary physical residence of the children.

     B.   Mary, Tom and the children have a successful, practical access schedule which will continue. Therefore, they have no interest in delineating that schedule in this document.

     C.   For tax purposes, Tom will be claiming the children as exemptions on his Federal Tax Return.

II.   Child Support

Tom will pay to Mary $1,250.00 per month in child support until Sue goes to college.

III.   Spousal Support

     A.   Tom agrees to pay to Mary the sum of $3,000.00 per month for five (5) years. Alimony payments will begin on the date of the final divorce decree and be paid each month thereafter.

     B.   Beginning in the year six (6) (the 61st month) and continuing through to the end of the year nine (9) (the 108th month) Tom agrees to pay $4,000.00 per month to Mary.

     C.   Alimony will cease after the 108th payment.

IV.   Property and Asset Distribution

     A.   Tom and Mary own commercial real estate properties as listed in Appendix A.

         1.   Mary shall maintain a 50 percent interest share in Tom's ownership of the properties. Mary's interest is financial, only, as Tom will continue to make partner-

ship decisions regarding the day-to-day operations of that property. Tom will provide to Mary a yearly accounting of the property activity as well as ensure her receipt of any distribution of profits.

2. With respect to all other jointly held properties listed in Appendix A, Tom agrees to purchase Mary's interest in all of these remaining marital properties for a sum of $300,000. Tom will provide payment to Mary based on the following payment schedule:

    a. $100,000 within 30 days of the signing of the divorce agreement.

    b. $50,000 per year for the next four years due on the anniversary date of the agreement.

3. Upon the final payment of the $300,000 Mary relinquishes all claims to any ownership of any properties owned by Tom except the Plaza property. Furthermore, Tom will be solely responsible to pay any debt owed on any of the remaining properties and will indemnify and hold Mary harmless from any cost to him by his failure to do so.

V. Pension and Profit Sharing

Tom currently has a Pension and Profit Sharing plan with his business which is valued at $500,000.00. Mary shall receive 50 percent of the assets of that plan which she shall "roll over" into her own pension account. The legal documents necessary for that will be proposed by her attorney.

VI. #1 Home and Lot

In the event of the sale of the marital home and additional lot, Mary and Tom agree to split the net profit of that sale on a 50/50 basis. Since Mary and Tom will be selling this property at a net loss, there are no other tax consequences to be considered.

VII. #2 Property Account

Mary and Tom have agreed to utilize the funds available in the #2 Property account to pay for any remaining bills associated with the mediation of the divorce. Any monies remaining in this account at the time of the finalization of the divorce shall be distributed to Mary.

VIII. IRA Accounts

As of the date of the divorce, the various IRA accounts of Tom and Mary listed at the end of this agreement shall be valued and each person shall receive an equal dollar value. The option of "rolling over" funds to an existing retirement account may be used by Mary if she so desires. Her attorney shall prepare any necessary Qualified Domestic Relations Orders.

IX.   Bank Stock

Tom currently has 100 shares of Bank Stock. Mary is to receive 50 percent of these shares of stock. She agrees that if she decides to sell any or all of her shares, Tom will have the first right to purchase her shares at the fair market value of the stock at that time.

X.   Health Insurance

Tom agrees to maintain his current health insurance coverage of the children until such time as they are no longer dependents. He also agrees to provide health insurance coverage for Mary until she completes her undergraduate degree or for 30 months, whichever comes first.

XI.   Life Insurance

Tom agrees to maintain his current life insurance policy with a face value of said policy of $1,000,000.00, naming Mary and the children as beneficiaries.

XII. College Education

Tom agrees to be solely responsible for the financial commitments of his two children's college educations.

XIII. Household Items

Mary retains sole ownership of all personal household items remaining in the marital home.

XIV. Business

Mary relinquishes any claim to assets or ownership in Tom's corporation. Similarly, Tom agrees to indemnify and hold harmless Mary for any debts or obligations associated with the corporation.

XV. Automobiles

Tom and Mary will each keep individual ownership of their present vehicles.

XVI. In the event of Tom's death, he agrees to prepare his will in such a way as to provide for the following options.

A. The continued "buy out" of the properties as set forth in paragraph III.

B. To provide for trust funds for each of the children in order to maintain their current support and educational needs.

C. To provide to Mary the net difference in cash between the amount of alimony paid to date and the total amount of $372,000.00 which would have been paid to her over the nine year term.

D. Prior to the finalization of the divorce, Tom shall provide to Mary a copy of his Will delineating the plan by which he will provide for options A, B, and C above.

Tom and Mary agree that in the event that there is a future dispute over the interpretation or dispensation of this agreement, prior to initiating any legal action, they will enter mediation in order to attempt to resolve said dispute. In the event the problems cannot be resolved in that manner, both parties reserve that right to initiate legal action.

MEMORANDUM OF UNDERSTANDING

Wanda and Lloyd Banks are dedicated to working together in the pursuit of the best interests of their son, Ryan. To that end, they have come to the following agreements regarding the parenting of Ryan:

1. Each parent's time with Ryan is valuable and toward that end they agree to respect each others time with him. They agree to share their time with Ryan as much as possible.

2. Wanda and Lloyd recognize that a shared legal and physical custodial arrangement is best for Ryan. Both parents agree to encourage Ryan to respect the plan they have worked out to share their parenting responsibilities.

3. Both parents agree that it is in Ryan's best interest to spend the school year with Wanda until the school year following his 12th birthday. Wanda and Lloyd further agree that beginning in the next school year and continuing through his high school graduation Ryan will be in the custody of his father during the school year. They believe that this arrangement is in Ryan's best interest and will proceed with that plan unless either parent becomes unable to care for Ryan, or if Ryan experiences significant medical or psychological problems which require a re-thinking of this plan.

Towards that end, both parents agree that until age 12 Ryan will reside primarily with Wanda during the school months and with Lloyd during the summer months. After age 12, Ryan will reside primarily with Lloyd during the school months and with Wanda during the summer months.

4. Both parents agree to include each other in decisions affecting Ryan's life including, but not limited to, his education, extra-curricular activities, medical treatment, religious upbringing and social needs. Both parents agree that it is important for them to honor this objective consistently in order to prevent alienation of parent from parent and/or parent from child.

5. Both parents agree to communicate with one another in a respectful manner, without the use of vulgarity and degrading terms, or arrogant and condescending attitude.

6. Both parents agree not to make any disparaging remarks about the other or the other parent's extended family members (including step-family, if any) in Ryan's presence. They also agree not to allow their family members to make any disparaging comments about the other parent in front of Ryan.

7. Lloyd and Wanda are committed to improving their communication and problem-solving regarding Ryan. To that end, they agree to identify a mediator with whom they can work. Initially, they agree to have, at least, two in-person meetings per year with the mediator. The expenses of those two sessions will be shared equally. In the event either parent needs an additional mediation session, the other parent agrees to attend. However, the expense of the session shall be the responsibility of the initiating parent.

8. With respect to time with Lloyd during the school year and summer while Ryan is in his mother's custody for the school year, the following arrangements shall be in effect.

   A. Thanksgiving shall be spent with Lloyd in all even years. The Thanksgiving Holiday shall be defined as beginning on the Saturday preceding Thanksgiving and continuing until the Sunday after Thanksgiving.

   B. Christmas shall be spent with Lloyd in all odd years. The Christmas Holiday shall be defined beginning on the day that school adjourns and continuing until the day before school resumes.

C. Spring Break is a time period during which Ryan will be with Lloyd each year until Ryan is 12 years old. The spring break will consist of a period of ten consecutive calendar days which shall be arranged around the period of time designated in the school year as "spring break" on the school calendar in the school in which Ryan is registered. The parents shall work together to arrange this time period so that Ryan misses the least amount of school possible. It is understood that Wanda will travel in both directions with Ryan for this access period.

D. Summer Access

1. Wanda shall deliver Ryan to Lloyd within 2 days after the last day of school for the year.

2. Ryan will return to the school year custodial parent 10 days prior to the 1st day of school of the new school year. However, for the summer of 2001, Ryan will return to Wanda 2 weeks prior to the beginning of the school year. Lloyd shall be responsible for traveling with Ryan at the end of the summer.

3. The non-custodial parent is entitled to a visit that will not exceed 7 days with Ryan during the summer. The visit will take place in the area in which Ryan is residing for the summer. Any other summer access is dependent upon the mutual agreement of the parents. The non-custodial parent will notify the custodial parent regarding the 7 day visit at least 6 weeks prior to the visit.

E. The non-custodial parent reserves the right to visit Ryan for up to 10 days during the school year. At least two weeks notice should be given to the custodial parent regarding the specific days of the intended visit. Additionally, the non-custodial parent agrees to insure that Ryan attends all school and extra-curricular activities while they are exercising their partial custody.

9. With respect to travel expenses, Wanda has agreed to request funds from her mother's Trust in order to provide the initial $4000.00 for all travel expenses involved in transporting Ryan to each parent. Any expenses exceeding the $4000.00 will be shared equally between the parents. Each parent shall have an opportunity to suggest travel arrangements which may prove to be more reasonable in cost as long as the travel times are not inconvenient for the child considering the child's age and other needs or violates the terms of this agreement.

10. Lloyd agrees to be responsible for 50% of the tuition for Ryan's private school each year, regardless of the location of the school, i.e. East or West coast.

11. With respect to telephone contact, each parent shall be entitled to reasonable telephone contact when the child is with the other parent. The custodial parent shall make every effort to allow the child to speak with the non-custodial parent at the time the non-custodial parent initiates the telephone contact. The custodial parent shall provide the non-custodial parent with the telephone number and location of where the child will be if the child would not be in the custodial parent's primary residence for more than a 24 hour period.

12. The parents agree that each non-custodial parent shall be entitled to other periods of partial physical custody as the parties may agree including, but not limited to, holidays and Ryan's birthday.

Notes

INTRODUCTION

1. Jerome T. Barrett, "The Psychology of a Mediator." Society of Professionals in Dispute Resolution, Washington, D.C., 1983. Occasional paper no. 83–1, unpaginated.

CHAPTER ONE

1. Jerold S. Auerbach, *Justice Without Law?* New York: Oxford University Press, 1983, p. viii.

2. Paul Wahrhaftig, "Nonprofessional Conflict Resolution." In Joseph E. Palenski and Harold M. Launer (eds.), *Mediation Contexts and Challenges*. Springfield, Ill.: Charles C. Thomas, 1986, p. 47.

3. Kenneth Cloke, "Politics and Values in Mediation: The Chinese Experience." *Mediation Quarterly*, 1987, *17*, 69.

4. Auerbach, p. 25.

5. R. F. Cook, J. A. Roehl, and D. Sheppard, *Neighborhood Justice Centers Field Test: Final Evaluation Report, Executive Summary*. Washington, D.C.: Government Printing Office, 1980, p. 7.

6. Cook, Roehl, and Sheppard, p. 15.

7. *Dispute Resolution Act, Statutes at Large* 94, sec. 17 (1980), *U.S. Code*, vol. 28, sec. 2(a)(5).

8. Nancy H. Rogers and Richard A. Salem, *A Student's Guide to Mediation and the Law*. New York: Matthew Bender, 1987, p. 13.

9. Anne Richan, "Developing and Funding Community Dispute Settlement Programs." *Mediation Quarterly*, 1984, *5*, 79.

CHAPTER TWO

1. Some of these factors were originally adapted from *A Student's Guide to Mediation and the Law*, by Nancy H. Rogers and Richard A. Salem. New York: Matthew Bender, 1987.

2. Jack Ethridge, "Mending Fences: Mediation in the Community." In Levin and others (eds.), *Dispute Resolution Devices in a Democratic Society*. Final Report of the 1985 Chief Justice Earl Warren Conference on Advocacy in the United States. Washington, D.C.: The Roscoe Pound-American Trial Lawyers Foundation, 1985, p. 76.

3. David M. Trubek and others, "The Costs of Ordinary Litigation" *U.C.L.A. Law Review*, 1983, *31*, 9.

4. Joe R. Greenhill, "State of the Judiciary Message." Quoted in Judy Kurth Dougherty, "Family Mediation—What Does It Mean for Lawyers?" *Texas Bar Journal*, Jan. 1998, *51*(1), 31.

5. Robert Coulson, "Remarks to the Fifteenth Anniversary Luncheon of the Center for Dispute Settlement." Rochester, N.Y., Sept. 27, 1988.

CHAPTER THREE

1. *Community Mediation in Massachusetts, 1975–1985*, Salem: Administrative Office of the District Court, 1986, p. 29.

2. Craig McEwen and Richard Maiman, "Small Claims Mediation in Maine: An Empirical Assessment." *Maine Law Review*, 1981, *33*, 237.

CHAPTER FOUR

1. For his insight on this issue, I especially thank James Melamed, founder of the Mediation Center, Inc., in Eugene, Oregon. Jim is an

active mediator, handling everything from divorces to complex civil disputes, as well as a teacher and trainer. Since 1983, he estimates he has formally trained more than 1,400 mediators. Even when I do not directly quote him, I am indebted to Jim for his contributions to this chapter.

2. Jerome T. Barrett, "The Psychology of a Mediator." Society of Professionals in Dispute Resolution, Washington, D.C., 1983. Occasional paper no. 83–1, unpaginated.

3. Michael Lang, personal communication, December 11, 1999.

4. Deborah M. Kolb & Associates, *When Talk Works*. San Francisco: Jossey-Bass, 1997, p. 486.

5. Kolb, *When Talk Works*, p. 484.

About the Author

PETER LOVENHEIM is a mediator, writer, and attorney. He is author of two previous books on conflict resolution, *Mediate, Don't Litigate* (1989), rated "excellent" by *Library Journal,* and *How to Mediate Your Dispute* (1996), rated among "Best Legal Reference Books" by *Law Library Journal.* His articles and essays have appeared in the *New York Times, New York* magazine, *Moment* magazine, and other publications.

Lovenheim was trained and certified as a mediator at the Center for Dispute Settlement in Rochester, New York, in 1985 and later served as that center's staff attorney and program director. In 1999, he received the Lifetime Commitment Recognition Award from the Center for Dispute Settlement.

In 1990, Lovenheim founded Empire Mediation & Arbitration, Inc., a private dispute resolution company offering services to the legal and business communities and to individuals across New York State. In addition to handling legal, commercial, and interpersonal cases, Empire has provided mediator training for federal and state courts and bar associations.

Lovenheim earned a B.S. degree in journalism, summa cum laude, from Boston University (1975) and a law degree from Cornell Law

School (1978). He has been a member of the bar of New York State since 1979, and for ten years he served on the Alternative Dispute Resolution Committee of the Monroe County Bar Association. Mr. Lovenheim is experienced in print and broadcast media and has appeared on "Larry King Radio," CNBC-TV's "Smart Money," Fox-TV (NYC-Channel 5), New York-1 Cable, and more than fifty radio programs nationally. He created and has taught the seminar, "Career Opportunities in Mediation," at the Chautauqua Institution in Chautauqua, New York, at statewide mediation conferences, and at other forums.

Index

College and university degree programs, 118–124; cost of, 117–118, 121; on environmental and public policy disputes, 116; examples of, 118–122; graduates of, careers of, 119, 121; pros and cons of, 122–124; resource information for, 122; teaching jobs in, 169–171, 182, 184–185

Colorado Office of Dispute Resolution, 204

Columbia College, 122

Columbia University, Teachers College, 122

Co-mediation apprenticeship, 109–110

Commending parties, for engaging in mediation, 16

Commercial dispute mediation, 33–34; attendees of, 14; examples of, 34; as independent private practice, 162–163; job opportunities in, 141–146; on-line, 146–150; referral sources for, 98; self-marketing of, 98; session length for, 11; settlement agreement for, 28–29

Common Ground, 204

Communication skills exercises, 107

Community mediation centers, 52–54; administrative jobs in, 172–174; case mix of, 34, 35, 44, 52, 53; development jobs in, 180–181; diversity in, 105; fees and stipends of, 40, 54, 129, 130–131; growth in, 9; mediation job opportunities in, 128–129, 130–131; mediation process in, 11–15; mediation support jobs in, 169; mediator background and qualifications in, 52, 54–56, 128–129; names of, 52–53; physical setting of, 11; resource information for finding, 54, 131; settlement agreements in, 26–27; special programs of, 53–54; speed of, 41; trainer positions at, 183–184;

training and apprenticeships in, 53, 102–110, 124, 129, 183

Community Relations Service, U.S. Department of Justice, 7; job opportunities at, 139–140

Community relations specialist, 180–181

Compensation or fees: for administrative positions, 173; for case managers, 171, 177, 179; for community mediation center services, 54, 129, 130–131; for court-connected civil case mediators, 58, 129, 131–133; for federal agency mediators, 138–139, 140; for independent divorce and family mediators, 69, 129, 153, 155; for independent general mediators, 129, 163, 164; for independent private mediators, 69, 129; for independent specialty mediators, 72, 129, 158–159, 160–161; locale and, 153; for mediation support jobs, 171; as motivation to become a mediator, 83–84, 85–86; for on-line mediators, 146, 148, 149; for private dispute resolution companies, 65, 129, 142, 143, 145; for sales and development jobs, 171, 180, 181; standards of conduct regarding, 201; in various settings, compared, 129

Competence, mediator, 197–198

Competition, of independent mediators, 115, 151, 155, 159–160

Compromise, 3; as settlement option, 23

Conciliation, as dispute resolution technique, 6, 107

Confidentiality: in caucusing, 22; explaining, in opening statement, 18; mediator's ability to keep, 88, 94; as reason to mediate *versus* litigate, 39–40; standards of, 198–199; training in, 108

Conflict exercises, 105–106

Conflict Resolution Center International, 212

Georgia: court-connected mediation in, 57; mediation office of, 205; Office of Dispute Resolution, 205

Goal statement, in opening remarks, 16–17

Good Shepherd Mediation Program, 183

Government mediation programs, 61–68; administrative jobs in, 174–175; background and qualifications for, 62–63, 128–129, 137, 138, 140; case types of, 52; compensation in, 129; federal, 61–63, 135–140, 174–175; mediation job opportunities in, 128–129, 135–141; mediation support jobs in, 169; mediator background in, 52; mediators in, 62–63; state, 63–64, 140–141, 175–176, 203–209; training for, 129

Graduate degree programs. See College and university degree programs

Greenhill, J. R., 40

Grynbaum, J., 72–73

GS (Government Service) pay scales, 136–137

H

Hale, K., 120

Harassment cases, 33, 44; in community mediation centers, 53

Harm prevention, mediation and, 44

Harvard Law School, Program on Negotiation, 122

Harvard School of Public health, 116

Hawaii Center for Alternative Dispute Resolution, 205

Health care dispute mediation training, 115–116

Health Care Panel, 66

Helper role, 88

Hidden conflicts, detecting, 109. See also Underlying issues

Hinckley, D., 71, 154–155

Hobbies, 130

Home Buyer/Home Seller Dispute Resolution Program, 75

Hostility: of litigation, 39; as reason for refusal to mediate, 12

Human resources mediation, 123

Humor, sense of, 95–96

I

ICANN, 150

Impartiality, 196

Independent private practice mediators, 9–10, 68–74; advantages of, 68–69; backgrounds of, 52, 128; break-even time for, 151; business guidelines for, 150–153; case types of, 52, 69; categories of, 69; divorce and family, 69–71, 83–84, 153–157; fees of, 69; general, 73, 128–129, 161–164; opportunities for, 128–129, 150–165; self-marketing of, 97–98, 151–153, 154, 157; specialty, 72–73, 153–161, 157–161. See also Divorce mediators; General mediators; Private dispute resolution companies

Independent trainers, 184

Indiana Conflict Resolution Institute, Indiana University, 205–206

Industrial relations trainers, 184

Information gathering, as prerequisite to mediation, 46

Initiation of mediation, 11–12

Institute for ADA Mediation, University of Louisville, 116

Insurance dispute mediation: attendees of, 14; as independent specialty, 160–161; on-line, 150; training in, 115–116

Intact relationship mediation, 32, 38–39

Intelligence, mediator, 93–94

Interagency ADR Working Group, 135

Interim agreements, 24

Internal Revenue Service (IRS), mediation program of, 61–62

International dispute mediation, 36

Internet, 117, 122, 146–147. See also On-line mediation

Proposal to mediate: agreement to mediate and, 11–13; timing of, 47–48

Prosecutor mediation programs, 61

Psychic cost, of being a mediator, 88–89

"Psychology of a Mediator, The" (Barrett), 88–89

Public mediation centers. *See* Community mediation centers; Government mediation programs

Public policy dispute mediation, 34, 36, 64; training for, 116

Puritans, 7

Q

Quakers, 122, 176

Qualifications, mediator. *See* Background and qualifications; Personality traits; Skills; Training

Quality of process, standards of, 199–200

Questions: for caucusing, 22–23; inviting, at beginning of session, 19

R

Racial dispute mediation: federal agencies for, 7, 139–140; specialized services for, 76–77

Real estate dispute mediation, 75; training in, 117

Realtors Association, 121

Record keeping, 109

Rectangular table, 15

REDRESS, 139

Referral lists: of court-connected mediators, 134–135; of government agencies, 63, 138; of private dispute resolution companies, 65–66. *See also* Panels

Referral sources: for business mediation cases, 98; for community mediation centers, 53; for independent divorce and family mediators, 69, 98, 153; for independent general mediators, 163–164; for indepen-

dent private mediators, 152–153; for independent specialty mediators, 157–158; for part-time mediators, 74; for private dispute resolution companies, 179. *See also* Court-connected mediation

Refusal to mediate, reasons for, 12, 43, 47–48

Regional dispute mediation, 36

Relationship, of mediator with parties, establishment of, 10, 19

Resolute Systems, Inc., 65, 216–217; contact information for, 216–217; mediator profile with, 67

Resolution Rooms, 148

Resolve, Inc., 217

Respondent, 8; engaging, in mediation, 12, 47–48; refusal of, reasons for, 12, 43, 47–48. *See also* Disputants

Restorative Justice Job Openings, Center for Peacemaking and Conflict Studies, Fresno Pacific University, 168

Results, overemphasis on, 86–87

Richan, A., 24

Ripe cases: over-, 46–47; under-, 45–46

Rogers, N. H., 20–21

Role plays, 90, 108–109

Roommate dispute mediation, 33

Rule-bending, 24

Rules of evidence, in litigation, 3, 19

Rules of mediation, 191–193

S

Sadat, A., 36

Safety, 38; mediator's calmness and, 92–93

Salem, R. A., 20–21

Sales Director position, 169

Sales jobs, 169–171, 179–182; background and qualifications for, 170; compensation for, 171, 180

Santa Barbara County, Superior Court, job notice, 132

Satisfaction rates, 7–8